CHANGING CHANNELS

CHANGING CHANNELS

FROM JUST THE FACTS
TO OUTRAGEOUS OPINIONS

JUDITH BISHOP

Palmetto Publishing Group
Charleston, SC

Changing Channels: From Just the Facts to Outrageous Opinions
Copyright © 2020 by Judith Monica Bishop
All rights reserved

First Edition

Printed in the United States

Hardcover: 978-1-64111-927-6
Paperback: 978-1-64111-931-3
eBook: 978-1-64112-061-6

For Eve, Ian, John, and Rose
My Fab Four

ACKNOWLEDGMENTS

Eternal thanks to those who supported me on the road to publication. Topping the list are my children Dana, Doug and Jack, and their wives Beth and Lauren.

One of my biggest supporters, global economist and author Nick Sargen, was a believer from day one and encouraged me every step of the journey.

Special thanks to dear friends and colleagues Marnie Inskip, Consuelo Mack, Denise Richardson, and Gloria Rojas—wise women and veteran journalists who were generous sounding boards especially in the early stages when *CHANGING CHANNELS* was just an idea.

My manuscript made the transition from concept to reality with marketing and technical assistance from longtime friends Shari Leventhal, a talented media executive, and Shannon Devereaux Sanford, an accomplished author and professor.

Special thanks to Michael Sesling and his team at Transcription Services in Boston. They provided prompt and accurate turnarounds. And for expert computer advice, my thanks to Roger Diequez and Christian R. Bauman.

Working with the production and editorial teams at Palmetto Publishing was smooth sailing and I will always value their professionalism and creativity.

Finally my appreciation to master publicist, Judy Twersky, a consummate pro and close friend. She and her A-team Ken Siman and Jennifer Bristol did a great job spreading the news.

TABLE OF CONTENTS

PROLOGUE

CHANGING CHANNELS is a book about journalism told by journalists who live the story 24/7. Facing unique challenges posed by a unique president, cable news channels are at a crossroads. Just as viewers are changing channels to the one that best reflects their political beliefs, news channels are reassessing their strategies. For prominent anchors and reporters, the stakes are high. Their decisions are shaping the current state of TV news and impacting its future. More Americans get their news from television than any other news source. Viewers are fascinated by rapid-fire events reported by larger than life media personalities. Is this the golden age of post-Watergate journalism? Or have some newscasts morphed from "just the facts" to propaganda masquerading as journalism? Are reporters taking sides or speaking truth to power? The lines are blurred as a debate rages over the new rules of the game.

The spotlight intensifies every day as accusations of "fake news" are countered by journalists invoking the First Amendment. The fundamentals of Big J Journalism are threatened by a media-bashing circus that labels reporters "enemies of the people." Does the press have a duty to alter course if it fears our democracy is threatened? Have reporters been pushed too far by a politician who lies too much? How are journalists adjusting their routine strategies to cover a president who is anything but routine? Are networks simply "mad as hell and not going to take it anymore"? As this drama plays out, anchors and reporters who make the most noise often get the most attention. Who are the heroes and who are the villains? What impact is this relentless war on the press having on the public's right to know and our national psyche? And what happens next in the inevitable post-Trump world? Will broadcast journalism revert to the old normal or is this the new normal?

CHANGING CHANNELS explores this headline-driven phenomenon. It's about journalism—its present and its future—told by the people who know it best. Through exclusive interviews and little-known public statements, high-profile anchors, reporters, executives, and media critics weigh in and tell us what they really think when the cameras aren't rolling.

CHAPTER ONE

THE WAR ON TRUTH

Coronavirus changed everything—and changed nothing. While millions were quarantined at home or dying in overwhelmed hospitals, the antagonism between the president and the media accelerated. Donald Trump seized the opportunity to double down, and at a crucial moment when the country needed compassion and honesty, he unleashed new levels of narcissism and dishonesty. When lives were in jeopardy and truth really mattered, the president of the United States labeled the impending plague a media "hoax" and gleefully predicted "like a miracle it will disappear." It did not, nor did the persistent war on truth that dominated his campaign and tenure in the Oval Office.

Even casual observers of the body politic realize many politicians lie. It goes with the territory. Most political lies are calculated to win votes in a tight election or diffuse a lethal scandal. Every modern president has been caught in a whopper so consequential it's recorded in history books and becomes part of the political lexicon. Remember these golden oldies? George H.W. Bush: "Read my lips, no new taxes." Bill Clinton: "I did not have sexual relations with that woman." George W. Bush: "Mission accomplished." Barack Obama: "If you like your doctor, you can keep your doctor." But Donald Trump lies habitually. Is it a calculated political strategy or a personality disorder best left to psychiatrists to analyze? We may never know the answer to that question. But how the press deals with his litany of lies is fair game and worth exploring.

CNN's Jim Acosta was at the center of the media storm and wrote about it in his book *The Enemy of the People*. "This was no time to be intimidated. This was the time to ask hard questions…Trump has often twisted the truth, lied, and attacked those who would call out his falsehoods—most notably the national press corps…He has thrived in this upside-down, through the looking glass landscape because facts don't carry the same currency they once did."[1]

At a news briefing during the peak of the coronavirus pandemic, Acosta read direct quotes from the president downplaying its danger. The CNN correspondent asked Trump to reconcile his inaccurate predictions with the actual number of infections and fatalities. Acosta was not speculating, nor was he embellishing. He was simply reading Trump's words, but the president attacked him and characterized the questions as "nasty [and] snarky."

The Washington Post compiles a factual analysis of political lies and awards "Pinocchios" to repeat offenders in both parties. Throughout his career, Donald Trump played to win, and when it comes lies, he is the undisputed winner. As of May 2020, *The Washington Post* documented over eighteen thousand false or misleading claims about issues, opponents, and the media. That's *Guinness Book of Records* territory, a systematic war on truth so unsettling it propelled many

Americans into a vortex of Trump fatigue and complicated life for journalists trying to ascertain the truth.

Ted Koppel and Jeff Greenfield are two award-winning journalists with a century of combined experience at the very highest levels. Greenfield asked his longtime colleague, "So you're a reporter and you and your colleagues cover Donald Trump...And you come to the conclusion, among other things, that this man is a consistent pathological liar that's just different from the normal political dissembling. So, if they report that, is it bias? Or is it a conclusion based on evidence?" Koppel replied, "I think you have a conclusion based on evidence. Although having reporters rather than columnists or editorial writers call the president of the United States a liar," bothers Koppel who suggests, "Is it possible to write a story in which the conclusion is unmistakable without putting it in that language?"[2]

CNN's Chris Cuomo raised his profile during the Trump years, moving from early morning to primetime. Cuomo's signature tagline reflects the dilemma journalists are confronting. Cuomo opens his nightly program with the exhortation, "Let's get after it," a catchphrase he believes captures the moment. "This is not the time to passively interview officials...If you have a challenge, get after it. For us, the reason we started the show was that it is no longer a time to sit and listen. You have to test. You can't just let things be said. Be assertive. Be aggressive. But be decent."[3]

One of the most startling pronouncements on the subject of truth came on an uneventful Sunday morning when Trump's attorney, Rudolph Giuliani, appeared on *Meet the Press*. He shocked moderator Chuck Todd and the viewing public when he uttered the words, "Truth isn't truth."[4] The eye-popping dictum was part political doublespeak, part bumper sticker mentality, and sadly emblematic of the Trump administration. Giuliani's distortion of objective reality echoed another stunner on *Meet the Press* when presidential counselor Kellyanne Conway floated the theory of "alternative facts." This concerted war on truth was clearly set in motion by a president who demanded loyalty and expected subordinates to stick to the script whether it's true or false.

In the early days of the administration, Press Secretary Sean Spicer worked overtime to sell the party line about the size of the inaugural crowd despite photographic evidence to the contrary. During his brief tenure, Spicer dodged questions on a regular basis, and to some degree got away with it.

Newton Minnow is a paragon in the annals of television history. His 1961 speech calling television "a vast wasteland" is still quoted and hotly debated. The former chairman of the Federal Communications Commission is now urging a back-to-basics approach "for journalists and for their publishers, producers and editors. Follow up, have persistence, and focus on broken promises and unfinished stories. Take a day to substitute collaboration instead of competition with your colleagues. If one reporter asks a question that gets no answer, the next reporter should ask the same question again and again, and so on. If there is still no answer, or an attempt to change the subject, all journalists present should consider joint action such as a walkout so the cameras can show the American people how they are being misled."[5]

That never happened in the White House Briefing Room during Spicer's tenure or Sarah Sanders's reign. Sanders lasted longer at the podium possibly because she tap-danced faster. But her evasive deflections infuriated veteran reporters who thought they'd seen it all. April Ryan of National Urban Radio said, "Not only does she not have credibility, she lied...She should be let go.

She should be fired. When there's a lack of credibility, you have to start lopping heads off."[6]

Paige Williams wrote a lengthy profile of Sanders in *The New Yorker* with the surprising revelation that off camera many journalists "like her personally and find her to be helpful and reliable." But in the briefing room, "Sanders often appears to mistake journalism for stenography or cheerleading. She sometimes tells the media what to 'celebrate' such as the state of the economy. Sometimes, when confronted with the fact that reporting is often adversarial, she reflexively mentions courtesy, seemingly not understanding that journalism is an exercise in democracy not etiquette." Williams quotes an unnamed reporter who told her Sanders "has said things that aren't true from the podium and she, at times, has deflected questions in a way that was misleading. But I've never caught her in a lie one on one…[even though] she can be obfuscating and ridiculous at the podium. Both of those things are true at the same time."[7]

Ultimately, Sarah Sanders wasn't fired, but she did step down at the end of June 2019. Her departure didn't soften criticism from the media. Conservative columnist Max Boot bid her farewell with the words that she was "opaque and dishonest, representing a liar."[8]

Most Americans did not recognize the name of Sanders's successor and couldn't pick her out of a lineup, because Stephanie Grisham never held a White House press briefing. She was the administration's "invisible woman." In contrast, her successor, conservative firebrand Kayleigh McEnany, was a popular fixture on FOX and had the potential to become Donald Trump's perfect Minister of Disinformation.

Presidential press secretaries and high-level staffers come and go in a perpetual game of musical chairs. It's a ritual dance that fascinates and impacts the White House press corps. Behind the scenes, journalists deal with key staffers on a daily basis. Insiders are the ones who dispense sound bites, off-the-record tips, and access—all essential elements in getting the story. But the average voter doesn't care who survives and who's fired.

Chris Matthews, who hosted *Hardball* on MSNBC, covered legions of politicians and dealt with legions of spokespeople. He told me, "White House staffers are public officials. Though their loyalty is to the president, they should honor the Thomas Jefferson rule: the whole art of politics is the art of telling the truth...I worked daily to build a show on facts. I liked to say we were fact based and heat seeking."

For beat reporters who cover the White House, facts are more difficult to uncover when access is diminished or denied. In March 2019, the Trump administration put a lid on daily briefings and went dark, severely limiting the opportunity to ask questions, get answers, and illuminate truth. More than ever, journalists had to rely on confidential sources inside the White House. Larry Sabato has been analyzing all things political for decades. He is the founder and director of the Center for Politics at the University of Virginia. He says, "Even people Trump hates, like my friend Jim Acosta, have excellent sources. And, in a sense, it's a confessional for some of these aides. You know, they feel they can continue to serve in the White House, serve their country...and yet balance it by leaking things that put Trump in a bad light. I understand that, but you know, you're making a deal with the devil."

Jim Acosta spent a career cultivating sources. "I would be remiss if I didn't report on the sizable number of officials in government who have attempted to help me and other reporters...We can't name them or Trump would run them out town on a rail...But there were officials who understood our need to get to the bottom of the president's agenda...When they found the occasional whis-tleblower, the Trump people swept many of them out of their offi-cial positions as best they could, but they couldn't find them all...Trump likes to blast these anonymous sources as phony and 'fake news,' but I'm here to tell you, and President Trump knows this, these sources are as real as you and me."[9]

Working sources is more enterprising and more productive than simply covering a news conference where journalists are spoon-fed the party line. Officials in both parties usually come prepared and stay on message. The fine art of journalism is to dig deeper and uncover facts, not just regurgitate speeches. Matthew Yglesias, co-founder of VOX, is troubled when journalists just repeat adminis-tration lies online or elsewhere without labeling the information as false. "It's a no-brainer not to do this. When a public official makes a material misstatement of fact, you might want to do a story about the fact that he is lying or confused or ignorant or whatever you think is going on. But you don't just relay the misinformation...There are tough questions in journalism, but this one isn't remotely tough. And yet it happens all the time."[10]

Katy Tur, who covered the Trump campaign for NBC and MSNBC, agrees. "Information coming from a politician or his team, without being vetted by reporters, is little more than propaganda...We really have to start teaching journalism in elementary school. People don't even understand the basics of what we do anymore."[11]

At MSNBC, Nicolle Wallace deliberately cut away from Trump's remarks on September 25, 2019 during his first news con-ference after the impeachment inquiry was launched. She bluntly told viewers, "The president is not telling the truth."

Covering presidential statements used to be a simple decision for journalists, but not anymore. Jeff Zucker, who heads CNN, once felt an obligation to report what's actually happening even if some pronouncements are peppered with lies. "He is the president of the United States and when he speaks that is newsworthy and that is important. And, frankly, you don't always know what he's going to say or where he's going to go…And I also think it's equally import-ant for people to see it in real time, in fullness, what he's saying, how he's saying it, what his verbiage is and the like. So, look, I under-stand that sentiment of people who don't think we should take it… But it's our job in real time. Look, we've taken to fact-checking him in real time…When he was saying that the Emoluments Clause wasn't real…we put the Constitution of the United States on the screen because it is real…We don't set out to be pro-Trump. We don't set out to be anti-Trump. We set out to be pro-truth. Now, I understand in this day and age, being pro-truth can be construed as being anti-Trump, but that's not our problem. That's not our fault. We're just here to ferret out the truth."[12] However, in the spring of 2020, as the Trump administration tackled coronavirus, CNN changed its approach and opted to dip in and out of live briefings omitting portions it deemed dishonest, irrelevant or blatantly par-tisan. Reporters had access to a president eager to pontificate but declined to broadcast every moment.

Looking back to an earlier period when President Trump curtailed formal news conferences, access was denied and reporters were forced to engage him as he walked across the White House lawn to a noisy helicopter. Being too passive was a danger, and so was be-ing too aggressive. Larry Sabato thinks reporters "have a Hobson's choice. They either participate in these shout fests and therefore look terrible to people who don't understand how the system works...They look rude...So what do they do? I mean, you can talk about boycotting, but that just means that we're left with tweets—tweets and official statements from obnoxious people in the White House. I mean, it's hopeless. It's hopeless. It really is. I don't know how fast it will improve."

White House correspondents like Jim Acosta struggle with that Hobson's choice every day. "Do we just absorb Trump's attacks? Or do we push back and stand up for ourselves? It's a difficult decision...In my view, Trump represented a new kind of president, one that required a different playbook for journalists."[13]

Former *CBS Evening News* anchor and current *60 Minutes* correspondent Scott Pelley wrote "a climate where what is false can be made to seem true and what is true can be made to seem false." He thinks we've moved "from the information age to the disinformation age." Some of that disinformation comes from new media (Facebook and other digital platforms) rather than old media (television, radio and newspapers) ...But the rules of content never change. With every story, the journalist asks: Is it right? Is it fair? Is it honest? Have I double-checked the facts with a skeptical mind? Have I balanced a variety of views? Have I written impartially, without placing my thumb on the scale of opinion? Journalism has much in common with the scientific method. In reporting, we don't care what the results are as long as they are true. The principles of honest content have not changed in a hundred years whether you're writing on a stone tablet or a glass tablet."[14]

One of the most comprehensive and perceptive analyses of the Trump versus Truth saga came from Derek Thompson at *The Atlantic*. The headline said it all: "Trump's Lies Are a Virus and News Organizations Are the Host." Thompson's theory is that "The president's conspiratorial language is an odious virus that has found a variety of hosts in the US media ecosystem. The traditional news media amplify his words for a variety of reasons, including newsworthiness (he is after all the president), easy ratings (cable news audiences soared in his term), and old-fashioned peer pressure (the segment producer's lament: 'If everybody else is carrying Trump, shouldn't we?'). But a virus doesn't just borrow a host's cellular factory to reproduce, it often destroys the host in the process."[15]

Derek Thompson doesn't just state the problem; he poses several solutions, including one called "the silent treatment. That solution is something like selective abstinence. Some journalists have adapted to the new normal by simply avoiding the president's language whenever possible." He quotes Rachel Maddow of MSNBC: "I don't go out of my way to play tape of the president speaking… The president very frequently says things that aren't true. He admits that he says things that aren't true. And I feel on this show I'd like you to be able to trust me to give you true information."[16]

Don Lemon of CNN takes the same basic approach when booking guests. He refuses to give some of the most outspoken Trump apologists a platform. "I never give a liar a platform because we have an obligation to tell the truth."[17] His CNN colleague and close friend Chris Cuomo disagrees. He believes that in fairness "We can't tune out the other side."[18] Case in point. Lemon is basically boycotting Kellyanne Conway, but she's appears on Cuomo's program, and when they engage, there's nothing "silent" about their sparring.

When coronavirus was peaking in March 2020 and journalists were weighing how to reconcile presidential lies with lifesaving information, there was radio silence at KUOW, the NPR station near Seattle. They continued to report on the epidemic but refused to air the daily presidential news briefings, citing "a pattern of false or misleading information that cannot be fact-checked in real time." The dramatic move was praised by some media critics and derided by others. Ted Koppel offered a cogent analysis in an email printed in the *New York Times*. "Training a camera on a live event, and just letting it play out is technology not journalism. Journalism requires editing and context...I recognize that presidential utterances occupy a unique category. Within that category, however, Donald Trump has created a special compartment all his own."

In addition to "the silent treatment," Derek Thompson quotes linguist George Lakoff, who advocates a strategy he calls a "truth sandwich." It's a three-step process that begins by stating the real facts, then quoting the lie, and finally restating the truth.[19] CNN's Kate Bolduan served up a "truth buffet" on the May 30, 2019 edition of her program *At This Hour*. The day before, Special Counsel Robert Mueller had broken his two-year silence and predictably Donald Trump reacted. Many of the president's assertions were demonstrably false and Bolduan set out to prove it. She tackled a variety of issues over the course of the program, including "no collusion" and the trade war. First she played Trump's comment, then expert panelists debunked each lie issue by issue.

Here's another innovative approach networks could easily employ, and it's fast and cheap. When any politician is obviously lying, they could print out the real fact on-screen as he or she is spouting the untruth. Hypothetically, if a candidate claims the Dow is up 28% and it's only up 16%, put that figure on-screen and source it. One picture can have a tremendous visual impact.

CNN tried a modified version of that by interviewing their in-house fact checker on air immediately after a lengthy presidential statement. It was an effective technique and a sad reminder of the dimensions of the problem.

The problem spun out of control when the coronavirus pandemic created a world of unintended consequences. In theory, daily presidential briefings were a good idea, a sensible way to keep the public informed. But in practice, they mutated into a media circus, a venue to lash out at opponents, settle scores, and beat the press with harsh invectives. At first, the cable news networks aired the availabilities from beginning to end regardless of length or content. It soon became apparent the incumbent president was using the forums to boost his reelection bid. The briefings became campaign infomercials, anemic substitutes for red-meat campaign rallies that were impossible during the era of social distancing. Eventually, CNN and MSNBC dipped in and out of the live briefings as information warranted. But there were other options.

Networks could have designated three edit rooms staffed by a producer and editor team who could take the feed and turn the tape. Each room could handle a specific segment. Make Team A responsible for the first fifteen minutes, Team B minutes 15–30, and Team C minutes 30–45. If it's a lengthy session, the process could cycle on a rotating basis as long as necessary. They'd simply screen and edit the feed, preserving all the relevant and accurate information while leaving lies and venom on the cutting room floor. As each segment was completed, the control room could roll the tape followed by live analysis from anchors and experts while the next segment was being crashed in another edit suite. Taking a "greatest hits" approach works because journalism inherently requires editorial judgment. It's not supposed to spread massive doses of misinformation, especially when people are dying at alarming rates from a virulent plague.

Another viable option might be the formation of a "Truth Squad," a rapid response team composed of retired and respected journalists—prestigious award winners who are generally regarded as impartial and experienced. They could remain above the fray because they're not actively covering the White House and confronting the president on a routine basis. The "Truth Squad" could immediately hit television and radio airwaves, setting the record straight and combating misinformation. One reason Donald Trump's lies are sticking is that they often fester unchallenged in the public discourse.

In the quest for truth, Dr. Larry Sabato urges journalists to rank presidential lies in categories. "I would put the minor lies on your website. Tell people you're putting it on the website so they can go and check it. Then focus on the big lies. They're the ones that matter…I think you have a better chance of capturing more of the audience and making them think about what this crazy president is saying and doing if you focus on the whoppers. And I don't mean the whoppers he serves athletic teams."

Ranking the importance of falsehoods may clarify issues for the public, but it would infuriate the president. On the campaign trail and in the Oval Office, Donald Trump reacted to negative headlines as monumental personal affronts. Even if the reporting was one hundred percent accurate, he ranted if reality didn't fit his narrative. His basic instinct was to attack, and that gave birth to the inflammatory mantra "fake news." Trump hammered it home in speeches, at press conferences, at fundraisers, and at rallies, where he whipped supporters into an anti-press frenzy. Chants of "fake news" filled auditoriums across the country and permeated cable newscasts. Then at daybreak Trump tweeted about "fake news," weaponizing his digital tirades. Platforms like Twitter present an ethical dilemma for journalists. When they repeat virulent tweets over and over, are they reporting the day's events or compounding the problem?

According to an in-depth survey, "For journalists who incorporate Twitter into their reporting routines, and those with fewer years of experience, Twitter has become so normalized that tweets were deemed equally newsworthy as headlines appearing to be from the AP newswire."[20] Equating Twitter and the venerable Associated Press says volumes about its impact on twenty-first-century journalism. Comparing angry civilians spouting disinformation with Pulitzer Prize winners has long-range perils for democracy and journalism.

Former CNN correspondent Frank Sesno was based in Washington with a bird's-eye view of presidents who governed in the world before Twitter. Viewing the current climate in historical context, he believes "Twitter can be a great tool or a great distraction. We see both. Certainly it has empowered this president and all others to go directly to the public. There's no bully pulpit like the presidency. And Trump has used Twitter to redefine the reach, the range, and the anger that he can use in amplifying his message. And he attacks any messenger who disagrees with him. Journalists should apply logic and proportionality to the importance they assign to tweet storms."

Assigning importance involves subjective choices. Journalists must decide: What to cover? When to cover it? How to cover it? Who to interview? Which sources to trust? How to verify facts? How much time to give the story? Does it lead the newscast? Or is it buried as the program winds down? Choices are an integral part of the process all day, every day. It's how the sausage gets made. But the key to those choices is fairness, not partisanship. Reporters should apply the same principles when they deal with Twitter. Does it serve the quest for truth to elevate Donald Trump's grumpy outbursts to headline status? It's tempting because the president's tweets are outrageous and compel viewers to stay tuned. He is the acknowledged Master of Spin, supremely adept at churning the political waters. Sometimes even veteran journalists who know better can't resist the bait. Trump's every utterance seems calculated to drum up controversy and keep his name front and center. Pete Vernon of the *Columbia Journalism Review* describes Trump's use of Twitter in a broader historical context. FDR used radio, JFK mastered television, and DJT is the undisputed King of Twitter.[21]

Supporters of President Trump relish his tweets, the more provocative the better. Early morning rants fire up the base and provide a road map for the day's conversation. And there's a valuable fringe benefit for the White House. If you repeat a lie often enough, it becomes part of the political vocabulary and gains the patina of truth. But it's not truth. It's not even spin or misrepresentation. It's lying. Donald Trump's most ardent supporters buy into the fiction, while many apathetic voters simply neglect to pay attention. However, defenders of all things digital argue Twitter has upsides. It's small "d" democratic, providing anyone with a computer an international platform to become a "citizen journalist." But think about this. Is creating "citizen journalists" really a good idea? No one has vetted their resumes, checked their references, and edited their copy. Would you want a "citizen dentist" or a "citizen neurosurgeon"?

In addition to the content of the tweet, readers also get a window into the mind of the tweeter. When that tweeter is the president of the United States, an intimate snapshot emerges. Brian Stelter of CNN's *Reliable Sources* thinks that "We learn an enormous amount about his mindset from his tweets…It's raw, shocking use of media by a president, like he's hosting a late-night talk show, picking fights, getting even with enemies…When I go on vacation and reinstall my account and see the president's Twitter feed, I can't help but be shocked by some of the things he shares...There's a numbness when his tweets come up in your feed day after day. I find it really useful to try and step away from it, to try and remember how extremely unusual this is."[22] But when he's back on the job, Brian Stelter believes journalists cannot take a hiatus. Presidential tweets are news and must be reported even when they're distasteful or divisive. Stelter's colleague, David Zurawik, media critic for *The Baltimore Sun*, agrees. "As journalists...we can't ignore him. You want to ignore him...God, I want to. Every time I see a tweet, I want to ignore it. We cannot do it."[23] April Ryan of American Urban Radio concurs. "As a White House correspondent, I cover everything presidential, so I cannot ignore the tweets even though I want to. Anything he says on Twitter or from a press release from whatever press secretary he has today, you have to look at that as the official word from the leader of this nation."[24]

Frank Sesno believes, "Many people are used to it. 'Don't take him literally,' they may say. 'Don't listen to each and every tweet. Look at the bigger picture—the judges, the immigration argument, the case he makes about America getting ripped off in an outsourced world.' But also, Trump was a reality TV star. He ran as a reality TV star. And though we call it reality TV, there really is precious little reality involved in this kind of made-for-media experience. So Trump's audience has built into their acceptance of him this sense of who and what he is. And then there's the 'credibility' of Trump's critics, be they Democrats, elites, or the press. They are out of step with much of America. So I guess you'd say everyone's credibility suffers in this environment."

It's supposed to be journalism 101 to red flag distortions from elected officials—and from media competitors when they cross the

line and present lies as facts. CNN's Brian Stelter cautioned viewers: "There are two news worlds— – FOX and everyone else…"
…FOX "is a Trump echo chamber."[25] Trump tweets. They report
with no context or corrections, effectively promulgating Donald
Trump's alternate reality.

Jeff Greenfield makes a similar observation. "FOX is an animal
we have never seen before to this extent. It is, in effect, state television that is reporting non-facts, which, by the way, go right into the
brain of the president of the United States, who apparently spends
hours of 'executive time' watching this." Ted Koppel takes that cri-
tique a giant step further. "I used to think that there was a sharp
distinction between FOX and MSNBC. There is still a distinction.
I still think that FOX is less adherent to facts and truth than they
are to really sharp political opinion. But the gap has been closing…
Ten, twelve years ago, NBC owned this little cable network that
was doing nothing, that had no ratings, was not making any money. And they look across the aisle to the folks at FOX, and FOX is
pulling down one-and-a-half billion dollars a year by catering to the
political appetite of people on the right side of the political spectrum. And somebody over at MSNBC had to have said, 'You know
something? Why don't we try that over on the left-hand side of the
spectrum?' And initially, it didn't do much, but gradually MSNBC
has become a powerhouse in its own right by doing what? By providing a mirror image to what FOX does. Do I like it any better on
either side? No, I really don't."[26]

If you're trying to monitor how the press weighs options and
makes decisions, Brian Stelter's *Reliable Sources* is an excellent way
to get the real story. His Sunday program is one stop shopping for
media junkies. Stelter's insights are on target and his guests are first
rate. Stelter believes Donald Trump's lies "are a sign of disrespect

for the public in general and his supporters in particular...When the press repeats his lies without clarification, we're making a bad situation worse...Why are we repeating lies?"[27]

CNN became a frequent target of the Trump administration. In response, CNN's president Jeff Zucker took a carefully measured approach when he issued a rare but strong statement. "Make no mistake, Mr. President, CNN does not lie." But CNN does push hard, especially their White House correspondent, Jim Acosta, who engaged in tenacious, monumental battles with the president and his spokespeople. Acosta admits his "confrontational approach created even more tension in the briefing room. A few reporters were starting to adopt the same practice of shouting out questions and turning to Twitter to take the press secretary to task. Of course, colleagues from other outlets, I'm fully aware, were rolling their eyes, annoyed by some of those tactics. There were plenty of reporters out there who felt we needed to continue to play by the old rules, even as this administration took extraordinary steps to destroy the rule book." Acosta says he got support, not criticism, from network brass. "Jeff (Zucker), to his credit, has never tried to control what I do as a reporter. I can't say that about a lot of TV executives."[28]

NBC network was also front and center on the presidential hot seat. At one point, Donald Trump accused Lester Holt, the respected anchor of *NBC Nightly News*, of distorting his comments about firing FBI Director James Comey. In an exclusive interview with Holt, the president clearly linked Comey's termination to Robert Mueller's Russia investigation. Even a high school media student could see the tape was not doctored. The camera remained on Trump for the duration of the contested comment. There were no cutaway shots of Holt, no opportunities to cut and paste, no opportunities to edit and distort. In this case, what you see is what you get—truth is truth.

As a candidate, Donald Trump was quick to figure out relentless repetition can transform outright lies into "false truths"—statements his supporters believe and echo. Why do they buy the snake oil? For the same reasons voters traditionally do. They hear what they want to hear. Some voters use political rhetoric as an excuse to mask racism or xenophobia. Others buy into fantasies because they're not sophisticated enough to discern fact from fiction. Others simply crave a generous tax break. Regardless of the cause, the effect has consequences in our national dialogue and at the polls. Trump's lies may be morally dishonest, but they're strategically honed and highly effective political ammunition that translates into votes.

Frank Senso points out, "For all the noise and criticism and second-guessing, and from the earliest days of this country, we invited the free challenge of ideas. No one has been immune from that. It's what makes us who we are. Ironically, it's also how Donald Trump catapulted to power attacking other politicians, using the media megaphone to be heard, capitalizing on missteps and inconsistencies to make his argument." That raises a troubling question. To what degree did the media's nonstop coverage of candidate Trump contribute to his eventual victory in 2016? Did the quest for ratings become in-kind campaign contributions?

"The media obsession with Trump during the primaries meant that the Republican race was afforded far more coverage than the Democratic race, even though [the Democratic race] lasted five weeks longer. The Republican contest got 63 percent of the total coverage between January 1 and June 7, compared with the Democrats' 37 percent."[29]

Katy Tur wrote, "Yes, we gave Trump a ton of airtime and article space. But that's because he's unlike anything anyone has ever seen.

And despite what folks who don't like him may want to argue, he is resonating. And we have an obligation to document it."[30]

Dr. Larry Sabato surveyed television coverage of the 2016 campaign and concluded all networks share some degree of blame. Now he believes, "CNN is compensating for what they did. It's penance for what they did in 2016. And I know why they did it. You know why they did it?…It's not that they thought that Hillary Clinton was ideal or perfect or anything like that. Some of them had giant fights with her. But they looked at the Republican field and figured if anybody will lose, it's got to be Donald Trump. They thought he would be interesting and so it would be the best of both worlds. You're not going to make him president, but he's going to create lots of time (and ratings and money) for you. I understand why they did what they did, but they absolutely helped him. And the other networks, I'm sure they participated. FOX obviously didn't want him at first. They were very opposed to Donald Trump, but they switched because they adjusted to reality. He was going to get the Republican nomination. And once they switched, they switched into full gear for Trump as they would have for any Republican nominee. Plus they discovered early that Trump would build their audience for all of the shows. They have made out like gangbusters because of Trump…Television is addicted to the candidates who spin great sound bites."

CNN's Jeffrey Toobin told me, "Yes, there was some excessive attention to Trump in the primaries, especially on cable. But I think the coverage improved a lot as soon as he became the de facto nominee." Looking ahead to 2020, Toobin says, "I don't know that formal limits should be imposed—just the application of sound journalistic judgment to each story that arises."

While the time-honored code of journalism is to gather facts and illuminate truth, reporting is a competitive business and the prevailing mantra is "get it first and get it right." A spirited tug-of-war between reporters and candidates is nothing new, but it reached unprecedented frenzy when Donald Trump descended the escalator and ascended to power. On his road to the White House, yes, the media made mistakes and some journalists got something wrong in the race to get it first. One study released by the Poynter Institute for Media Studies had a banner headline "Not Fake News: Just Plain Wrong." In a 24/7 news cycle, the pressures are intense to get on the air fast and say something that resembles real reporting even if it's based on precious little solid information.

CBS veteran Scott Pelley notes, "Among the worst self-inflicted wounds in journalism is the headlong rush to be first with a story. Ironically, this has no value whatsoever to the audience. It is a narcissistic game we play in our control rooms as we keep score among the video monitors carrying coverage of our competitors. Our audience would prefer we be right rather than first."[31]

Pelley makes an excellent point. Hypothetically, if you're home watching your favorite news channel and they report a breaking story two minutes after the competition, you don't know that. You're only watching one station, not a bank of monitors. The "race" is primarily inside baseball, a perennial contest of industry one-upmanship that has little currency in the real world.

Katy Tur, who was assigned to cover candidate Trump on the 2016 campaign trail, revealed what happened behind the scenes, citing relentless pressure to report as a story was developing before all the facts were clear. She did more than 3,800 live hits on MSNBC and NBC. Tur was strong enough, smart enough, and lucky enough to survive. But getting tossed into the lion's den unprepared can be a career ender.

Jim Acosta wrote about this potentially devastating trap. "As my colleagues and I were reporting on the latest twists and turns…it felt we were stepping carefully across a minefield. One small screwup and Trump would call us 'fake news.' We were constantly aware of that danger."[32]

Several news organizations made mistakes and paid the price. ABC News corrected its erroneous report alleging General Michael Flynn violated the Logan Act during the 2016 campaign. Investigative icon Brian Ross was suspended and eventually left the network after a stellar career that had spanned decades. A CNN report about sanctions erroneously linked Anthony Scaramucci to a Russian investment fund. In the aftermath, three journalists resigned. FOX aired false conspiracy theories surrounding the death of DNC staffer Seth Rich, but no heads rolled.

When individual reporters make mistakes or express bias, it gives the entire press corps a black eye. Other journalists have an instinctive reaction to close ranks like police officers erecting a "blue wall" of silence. Reporters feel they're getting enough criticism from the White House and don't want to cannibalize each other. But sometimes, a reporter breaks ranks and speaks out. Former *60 Minutes* correspondent Lara Logan spoke out. "There is nothing more human than opinions and bias. To say we have none is dishonest. But what we do have as professional journalists is a simple standard to get us past that—two firsthand sources, question everything and independently verify. I didn't invent this. I inherited it from people like Edward R. Murrow and I will keep passing it on."[33]

CNN host Chris Cuomo addressed the question of bias, acknowledging that the potential to manipulate your audience is a major pitfall. "I think there's no question that the audience is

THE WAR ON TRUTH

influenced and that's why you have to be responsible about what you do with the trust they're giving you by coming and listening to you and taking you seriously. But you don't report to influence outcome…I don't test people hoping they think something. I just hope they think. Now, all right, you've seen this idea tested. You've seen what he or she was able to do under this kind of scrutiny. Now you decide."[34]

Lara Logan cautions, "Journalists are not activists. We may share a passion for a particular cause, but our job is to follow the facts wherever they may lead. We can't ignore something that reflects badly on a noble cause, as an activist might. We have to care about the means as much as the end because our duty is to search for the whole truth. Nor are we lawyers in a court of law cherry-picking facts to prove our case. Fortunately, there is only one truth. How we feel about it, how we perceive it, those things are subjective but the truth itself is not. Above all, we are not propagandists or political operatives. That is not our job."[35]

Without specifically referencing Logan, two esteemed veterans of ABC's *Nightline* essentially concurred with her analysis. Jeff Greenfield asked Ted Koppel, "Let's put FOX News aside for a moment…When you watch CNN or MSNBC for four hours at night, basically what you're getting is a clear editorial message about the fitness of the president." Koppel replied, "I think unambiguously, yes…I am in total accord with you…I don't know how journalism ever gets back to being what it once was if we accept the notion that people who are not editorial writers, people who are not opinion writers or columnists…are quite obviously tilted in the direction of what I think is somewhat grandiosely referred to as 'the resistance.' To me, the resistance is Paris in 1943. The resistance is Stalin's Russia."[36]

Greenfield agreed. "The same person who writes a news report in the morning then comes on CNN or FOX or wherever and expresses an opinion. There's a mixing of roles there." To which Koppel replied, "Even when that reporter doesn't express an opinion, he's sitting at a round table or sitting at a desk with three or four other people whose opinions are quite clearly and vehemently expressed every day; there's an element of that that rubs off...I'm not objecting to editorial opinion being expressed. But it seems to me that you undermine the capacity of the greater reading public or viewing public...to accept the objectivity of journalists once journalists become not just reporters of fact but also expressers of opinion."[37]

Pulitzer Prize winner Seymour Hersh also yearns for the good old days. "There were no televised panels of 'experts' and journalists on cable TV who began every sentence with the two deadliest words in the media world—'I think.' We are sodden with fake news, hyped-up and incomplete information, and false assertions delivered nonstop by our daily newspapers, our televisions, our online news agencies, our social media, and our president. Yes, it's a mess."[38]

Strong words from journalistic icons, men so prominent they're practically immune from criticism. But younger journalists discover speaking out against their peers is not popular. Lara Logan took a big risk when she voiced concerns. "I will be attacked...But I welcome these attacks because it tells me my words matter. And I speak on behalf of journalists who believe in standing up for the truth and honest, independent reporting. Most do not feel free to speak publicly. We live in a free country, yet as journalists we are not free."[39]

While reporters were reluctant to criticize each other, Donald Trump was taking names and poised to attack. Former aide Anthony Scaramucci told CNN that the president's instincts are excellent and he knows how to perceive weakness and when to counterpunch. He also knows that distorting the truth can generate votes for him personally and, by extension, for coattail Republicans. Scaramucci believes when candidate Trump hits the campaign trail, he goes into "performance mode" and puts on a "show" that wins votes the way *The Apprentice* won ratings. But that characterization echoes Machiavelli. Do we really want a leader whose primary virtue is expediency not honesty?

Blending fact and fiction was standard operating procedure for Donald Trump dating back to 1987 when he chronicled his rise to mogul status in *The Art of the Deal*. He bragged, "I play to people's fantasies…People want to believe that something is the biggest and the most spectacular. I call it truthful hyperbole. It's an innocent form of exaggeration—and a very effective form of promotion."

NBC's Katy Tur watched that gamesmanship play out at rally after rally in state after state. She wrote in her book *Unbelievable*, "People seem drawn to Trump's rallies in the same way that they're drawn to professional wrestling, and as with a professional wrestling match, they seem divided between people who believe all they see and hear and those who know it's partially a performance. The scariest thing about being at a Trump rally is you don't know who believes it and who doesn't."[40]

When I interviewed Margaret Sullivan, media columnist at *The Washington Post*, in late 2018, she said, "Even Trump's strongest supporters understand that he doesn't tell the truth, or often doesn't tell the truth. They seem to be OK with it. Some of them are. But the midterm elections can be seen, in part, as a repudiation of what President Trump stands for, and I think truthfulness is part of that." At that juncture, Sullivan was taking a measured approach. But as time passed and Donald Trump dodged impeachment conviction,

Sullivan concluded he was emboldened and "unbound." In a hard-hitting column, she wrote that when circumstances change methods sometimes have to change. "We need a new and better approach if we're going to do our jobs adequately. First, we need to abandon neutrality-at-all-costs journalism. To replace it with something more suited to the moment. Call it Fairness First...Second, we need to be far more direct in the way stories are put together and presented...We are simply not getting across the big picture or the urgency. This happens, in part, because those news organizations that haven't chosen sides—those who want to serve all Americans—fear being charged with bias. And so they soften the language. They blunt the impact...cautious to a fault, afraid of their own shadows, and worried about being labeled anti-Trump or biased...My prescription is less false equivalence, more high-impact language and more willingness to take a stand for democracy. With Trump unbound, the news media need to change. Yes, radically. The stakes are too high not to."

While Trump's lies are appalling, there's something equally appalling. Where are his Republican critics? With John McCain gone, there are few elected officials willing to lead a truth offensive or even participate in one. Mitch McConnell and Lindsey Graham guzzled the Kool-Aid. Paul Ryan counted the days until he got out of Dodge. Jeff Flake, Bob Corker, and Ben Sasse had their moments, but never sustained their attacks in a meaningful way. Former Ohio Governor John Kasich proved to be a reliable watchdog and occasionally so did Senator Mitt Romney. But in the effort to dispute Trump's lies, most elected Republicans were invisible enough to qualify for the witness protection program.

Ted Koppel points out that their passive acquiescence began during the 2016 campaign. "I assumed at some point the Republican party would step in. They would deny him the nomination or, when the *Access Hollywood* tape came out, I mean, they would say, 'You have to leave the ticket.' Or at some point, institutionally, the Republican senators would say, 'You know, you're doing an executive power grab. We don't care that you're a Republican. We're going to stop you.'...You have Susan Collins, you know, whipping out her thesaurus. 'I'm distressed. I'm upset. I'm discomfited. I'm worried. I have agita.' And that's about it."[41]

Larry Sabato at the University of Virginia is also troubled by the lack of meaningful response by GOP officials. "Almost anybody with an R next to their name gives Trump a pass on almost everything...Given the choice between being in the next edition of *Profiles in Courage* or maintaining their power and position by being cowards, they've chosen the latter, almost all of them."

While most GOP elected officials were MIA, conservative media elite spoke up, signaling they're more committed to patriotism than party. Notable voices include Max Boot, Bill Kristol, Mark McKinnon, Peggy Noonan, Steve Schmidt, Michael Steele, Nicolle Wallace, George Will, and Rick Wilson. Their criticism of Donald Trump's aversion to truth was principled and harsh.

Most television hosts at FOX toed the party line regardless of the facts. But Chris Wallace, Shepard Smith, and Bret Baier were courageous exceptions willing to criticize President Trump when he veered out of bounds. Shep Smith, apparently fed up, shocked the media sphere when he abruptly resigned in October 2019. FOX colleague Neil Cavuto didn't resign, but he did offer a lengthy monologue addressed to the Commander in Chief. He said, "Let me be real clear, Mr. President. How can you drain the swamp if you're the one muddying the water?...I'm not saying you're a liar, I'm just having a devil of a time figuring out which news is fake. Let's just say your own words on lots of stuff give me, shall I say, lots of pause…None of this makes me a never-Trumper, just always confused…None of this makes you evil. But I am sure you can understand why even your friends say these inconsistencies don't make you look good…It's not just what you're omitting, Mr. President. It's what you keep stating and never correcting…I guess you've been so busy draining the swamp to ever stop and smell the stink you're creating."[42]

Washington Post columnist Max Boot went even further in his criticism of Donald Trump. In his book *The Corrosion of Conservatism: Why I Left the Right*, he wrote, "The Republicans used to be a conservative party with a racist fringe. Now they're a racist party with a conservative fringe." Considering his conservative credentials, Boot's assessment is both stunning and sad. But it wasn't surprising after the debacle at Charlottesville when President Trump gave white supremacists a free pass saying, "There were fine people on both sides." That presidential dictum prompted other lifelong Republicans to speak out on the potential for future violence. Republican strategist Rick Wilson said, "Of course President Trump encourages violence." Wilson believes Trump's statement was "not a dog whistle. It's an air raid siren."[43]

Reporting in the aftermath of Charlottesville was a tricky proposition. Calling the president of the United States a racist—or even implying it—is dangerous territory. Jim Acosta wrote about walking that fine line. "When it's a matter of right versus wrong, there are not two sides to the story…Who am I to judge whether he's gone off the deep end? I think that's fairly obvious. Whether it's an attack on the press or a blatant lie about policy or a betrayal of American principles (e.g. that Nazis are the scum of the earth), a more restrained reaction from a reporter sets a precedent that what has been said is now acceptable in our democracy."[44]

What's always been acceptable in our democracy is freedom of the press on the front page and diversity of opinion on the editorial page. Ted Koppel suggests if you really want to know what's going on in the world of political journalism, it's important to survey the broad spectrum of news outlets. He said, "I listen to Rush Limbaugh. I watch FOX. I really do want to know what is being said and there are some very good journalists on FOX. Chris Wallace, who is an old ABC colleague, does a fine job. Brit Hume does a fine job."[45] Doing a fine job resulted in criticism from the president, who taunted Chris Wallace with the ultimate Trumpian insult, "He should be on fake news CNN."

As the battle between the Oval Office and the media escalates, some critics are questioning the political affiliations of journalists. Are they registered Democrats or registered Republicans? Former *60 Minutes* correspondent Lara Logan, who now appears on the FOX News Channel, says "It's a fact that the vast majority of journalists in this country are registered Democrats. The colleges we come from are similarly dominated by one political ideology. This matters today because the reporting has become so one-sided. As we try to figure out why people have lost faith in our profession, let's start by being honest about who we are. I would feel the same way if the media were tilted in the opposite direction. It is the one-sided nature of this fight that disturbs me. Is that what the Founding Fathers had in mind when they wrote the First Amendment? We dismiss conservative media outlets for their political bias, but we don't hold liberal media to the same standard. Many journalists who claim to be objective have publicly taken a political stand, saying the urgency of the time justifies a departure from journalistic standards. Yet they ask us to believe their reporting is still unbiased."[46]

Katy Tur made a surprising admission in her book *Unbelievable*. "Like a lot of political reporters, I don't vote because I think it's fairer that way. We are not part of the campaign; we're observers of it. But that doesn't mean political reporters aren't poised to benefit if the candidate they cover goes all the way to the White House." [47] Nonvoting journalists like Tur believe riding a candidate's coattails to a higher-profile beat is an inherent conflict of interest.

Conservative podcaster Ben Shapiro is editor-in-chief of *The Daily Wire*. He suggests reporters declare their political party preference in advance so readers can gauge their degree of objectivity. [48] That's a revolutionary idea that probably won't and shouldn't gain much traction.

Ted Koppel said when he was a young correspondent, "Back in the 60's and 70's, did people think that reporters, television reporters, were probably more left of center than right of center? They've always thought that. But, in the final analysis, there was still a preparedness to accept that by and large they're trying to report the facts." Koppel asked Jeff Greenfield, "Let me ask you a question. In the final analysis, what do you think is the main reason we have hour after hour of coverage of essentially the same subject day after day? What's behind that, do you think?" Greenfield didn't skip a beat. "Money. Money." Koppel agreed. "Exactly. Exactly."[49]

Greenfield pointed to one of his alma maters, CNN, saying, "The critical mass of people who only wanted to hear about Trump and Mueller is why the third-ranking cable network CNN...is going to make a billion dollars. And second...it's a lot cheaper to bring people around a table than to send them off around the country with a camera covering the story."[50]

Many journalists agree covering Donald Trump presents a variety of difficult questions. How do you cover a president who's adept at changing the subject and diverting attention like a ring-master at a three-ring circus? How do you cover a president who constantly resets the agenda by creating false controversies and manufactured debates?

When I spoke with Margaret Sullivan of *The Washington Post*, she said the press bears some degree of responsibility for taking the bait. "I think the press, in general, has been too willing to let Donald Trump play de facto assignment editor. When he wants to talk about the dangers of immigration and focus on the caravan coming up through Mexico to the US southern border, we see a lot of press coverage of that, some of which is nuanced and smart and necessary. And some of which is just plain over-the-top. But it does seem as though he is able to change the subject, to give us a shiny-object distraction and keep journalists and the public from focusing on more substantial issues."

Even the deadly coronavirus didn't deter President Trump from changing the narrative. When the pandemic was peaking and he gathered the White House press corps for a daily five o'clock briefing (aka "the five o'clock follies"), he trotted out irrelevant administration officials who delivered progress reports on a variety of unrelated policies like the war on drugs and building the wall. Their performances were "warm-up acts" for the main event—medical superstars Doctors Anthony Fauci and Deborah Birx, who were there to address the real crisis and deliver lifesaving information.

Jim Acosta of CNN was quick to recognize this problem in the early stages of the administration. "Patterns began to emerge. The Trump tweets, hyperbolic, misspelled, factually challenged, would come in the morning, throwing off the news cycle...He would attack an adversary, real or imagined, and the narrative of the day would change again." [51]

Reaction was even harsher from Kyle Pope, editor-in-chief and publisher of the *Columbia Journalism Review*. "If the mission… was to keep Trump from leading us around by the nose, I'm afraid we have failed…The sad fact is that the current approach to covering this White House is no longer working…That requires a new journalistic enterprise, more creativity in terms of what form that journalism would take, a rethinking of how we tell our stories…We, as a profession, are capable of figuring this out…I think the answer likely lies in the seams between more conventional approaches to reporting. I want to see more first-person pieces by reporters on the trail, some oral histories, some theoretical what-ifs. Let's not leave the most truthful storytelling to fiction writers or dodgy book writers. This is an extraordinary moment and it requires a new, proactive urgency to tell the story of this presidency as we see it, rather than fall into the swirl of familiar tropes and outrages. But we're never going to do it if we continue to follow the lead of our dear leader who needs us nearly as desperately as we apparently need him."[52]

Donald Trump needed two things from the press corps—attention that he got in spades and exoneration on Russian collusion. Despite the carefully structured ambiguity of the Mueller Report, it's a safe bet something really was rotten in the state of Russia. Trump's Moscow connections date back three decades. Real estate mogul Donald Trump aspired to build a tower in Moscow, and that dream became his Moby Dick, sometimes within reach but always elusive. Trump's book *The Art of the Deal* was released in December 1987. At the time, I was producing a Sunday-morning political program on WABC TV in New York. It was called *Eyewitness News Conference* and Donald J. Trump was a high-profile guest. He was a charismatic talker who reliably doubled our ratings. At the time,

"The Donald" was a pop-culture figure in the Big Apple, named by *New York* magazine one of the most influential people in the city. We scheduled him to discuss his newly released autobiography that was destined for the bestseller list. Shortly before the taping, my telephone rang in the newsroom. It was Tony Schwartz, Trump's coauthor, who actually wrote the book. He said Trump would give us an exclusive if we "ask him about Russia." I responded, "We could ask the question, but first we need to know the answer." Schwartz said Trump was "going to build a hotel in Moscow near the Kremlin and would break the news on our program." That was the genesis of Donald Trump's Russian pipe dream—1987. He negotiated on and off for over thirty years. Who knows what transpired during that period? Who knows the truth about damaging kompromat— business or personal? To what degree was Donald Trump's Russian connection his sword of Damocles, overshadowing his rise to power and his fawning relationship with Vladimir Putin? That's a truth we may never know, shrouded in lies.

Donald Trump's lies extended beyond his desk in the Oval Office to his inner circle. Critics say he surrounded himself with a lair of liars. Was the penchant for lying contagious? Was it coincidence? Or did he deliberately seek out lieutenants who were ready and willing to deceive?

Jim Acosta points out, "Inside the Trump team, multiple aides told me, they were just fine with misleading the press. That was not the same as lying to federal prosecutors...As the lies mounted, it seemed too hard to write them off as coincidence." [53]

Some of President Trump's high-prolife deputies learned the hard way that telling the truth is not optional when speaking with federal prosecutors or testifying before Congress. If you don't stick to the facts, the alternative is perjury unless you "can't recall," a handy catchphrase that often implies consciousness of guilt. Assessing the veracity of Trump's acolytes, it's crucial to note that many of their lies involved Russia. Michael Flynn was a member of Trump's brain trust who was forced to resign because he lied to Vice President Mike Pence about meeting with a Russian ambassador. Months later, Flynn played liar's poker with the FBI and lost. Nevertheless, he had defenders. On FOX primetime, host Tucker Carlson reacted to the Flynn case by voicing exasperation with the slow pace of the Mueller investigation, saying, "If it's just a bunch of stupid perjury charges, someone should be punished."[54] Carlson was criticizing the feds, not the perjurer. Since when are perjury charges merely "stupid"? Only if you think it's OK to lie under oath.

One of the most insidious lies surfaced after the assassination of *Washington Post* columnist Jamal Khashoggi inside the Saudi Arabian Consulate in Istanbul. The CIA conducted an in-depth investigation and determined the plot was engineered by Crown Prince Mohammad bin Salman and executed by his personal hit squad. Andrea Mitchell of NBC and MSNBC said, "Despite the CIA'S conclusion...the president comes out, he's being pressed. What do you say about these conclusions? And finally he has to acknowledge he's studied them and he says, 'Well, they're not conclusive. Maybe he did it, maybe he didn't.' Literally that's what he said, 'Maybe he did it, maybe he didn't.'" Mitchell challenged the president's cold and calculated justification of murder. "So [he's saying] they're an ally and there are some things that are more important basically than human rights...Never before have we had a modern president who has said that human rights is not an American value...So we crossed a bar...This is not just a minor decision, in saying that our foreign policy is going to be determined by dollars, by oil, and by a shared opposition to Iran."[55]

In the aftermath of Khashoggi's murder, the dark art of dissembling extended to the president's cabinet. Even once-respected Secretary of Defense James Mattis and Secretary of State Mike Pompeo dodged the truth when they spoke to reporters in a joint appearance to shoot down the theory of bin Salman's treachery. It's impossible to know what motivated their distortion. Was it pressure from the Oval Office? Were they afraid of contradicting the boss and getting fired? Was it an overriding desire to maintain strategic relations with a Mideast powerhouse? Or was it all about oil? Trying to ascertain the real story, journalists had a very personal motivation to reveal the truth. Reporters often cover murders, but they rarely know the victim or count him a friend and colleague.

Another high-profile cabinet member, Attorney General William Barr, struggled to separate fact from fiction when he issued a four-page summary of the 448-page Mueller Report. When the Special Counsel testified before Congress and finally broke his silence, he called Barr's veracity into question. Mueller wrote, "The summary letter the [Justice] Department sent to Congress and released to the public late in the afternoon of March 24 did not fully capture the content, nature and conclusions of this office's work and conclusions." A subsequent letter from Mueller stated, 'There is now public confusion about critical aspects of the results of our investigation." Best-case scenario: Barr spun the facts in a devious, well-executed campaign to influence public opinion and cement the president's claims of "no collusion." Worst-case scenario: Barr lied and possibly committed perjury when he testified before Congress. His fiercest critics point out that Barr's lies escalated in tandem with the impeachment inquiry.

Somewhere between truth and falsehood lies the nebulous realm of "truthiness." Late-night host Stephen Colbert coined the term in

2005 in the world before President Trump. The *Oxford Dictionary* crowned "truthiness" Word of the Year and defined it as "The quality of seeming or being felt to be true even if not necessarily true." For "truthy" Americans, feelings and perception count—but facts do not. Sound familiar? Ted Koppel, who made a career telling the truth, believes "Stephen Colbert does a brilliant job every night. Bill Maher does a brilliant job." And Jeff Greenfield applauds "John Oliver, Samantha Bee and Trevor Noah," suggesting they have "taken over what journalists used to do." But Koppel reminds us, "What they do brilliantly is no more a substitute for good news coverage than a great editorial cartoonist like Herblock would have been a substitute for Woodward and Bernstein."[56] They were the heroes of Watergate. Who will be the heroes of Trumpgate?

Journalistic truth-seekers are doubling down and digging deep, but the jury is still out. CNN's Anderson Cooper digs deep every night on *AC 360*. "Truth...is under assault, facts are called fake, lies are used to divide us, to weaken confidence in journalism and the core institutions that are essential to maintaining our democracy. The answer in my mind to the attacks on reporting is more reporting."[57]

The dictionary definition of "truth" is simple: "The quality or state of being true in accordance with fact or reality." But when great thinkers defined "truth," it became nuanced with infinite shades of gray. Aristotle said, "The investigation of truth is in one way hard, in another way easy. The cause of the difficulty is not in the facts, but in us." Mahatma Gandhi believed, "There is no higher god than truth." Acclaimed Russian novelist Leo Tolstoy expressed his opinion poetically: "Truth like gold is to be obtained by washing away all that is not gold." Even musical icons tackled the subject. George Harrison said, "You can be standing right in front of the truth and not necessarily see it. People only get it when they're ready to get it." And centuries ago, when our country was in its infancy, Founding Fathers weighed in. Thomas Jefferson believed "Honesty is the first chapter in the book of wisdom," and George Washington said, "Truth will ultimately prevail where there is pains taken to bring it to light." That's exactly what journalism is supposed to do.

Navigating the Trumpian landscape, journalists had to adapt and figure out how to operate in a world where the president was running the country like a bizarre reality show. As Jeffrey Toobin of CNN put it, the Trump administration "started out as nonfiction, moved to fiction, then science fiction."[58]

The warning signs point to danger ahead—danger for the First Amendment and the public's right to know. What happens next? No one knows for certain, not even the people who live the story. Have journalists crossed a sacred line and ventured into the world of partisan opinion? Or are they the last bastion of hope in a vortex of political lies?

CHAPTER TWO

BATTLE OF THE TITANS

From day one, the presidency of Donald J. Trump was a slugfest. In one corner: the Titan of Pennsylvania Avenue. In the other corner: anyone who happened to raise his ire. But his favorite punching bag was the press. That was the main event. Every modern president sparred with the press, but during the reign of Trump the never-ending battle assumed titanic proportions, because Donald J. Trump reduces life to one simple equation. Who won and who lost? For him, "Winning isn't everything. It's the only thing."[59]

Confrontations have always been part of political journalism. During Watergate, relentless reports about Richard Nixon were broadcast nightly on the three major networks. Decades later, FOX attacked Barack Obama, demeaning him at every turn, even challenging his birth certificate. When the Founding Fathers crafted the First Amendment, they designated the fourth estate to check the three branches of government. But today many voters are turned off by the constant war of words and cast blame on politicians and reporters alike, saying they deserve each other and represent two sides of the same devalued currency. The irony is most members of the press don't want a knock-down, drag-out fight. They just want to do their jobs and expect a fair amount of valid criticism that goes with the territory, always has, and always will.

Chris Matthews, the outspoken former host of *Hardball*, told me he preferred not to slug it out. "I called it as I saw it. It was never personal...The challenge was to avoid developing an attitude towards Trump. You need to display your skepticism in your questions, not in your demeanor...Ask questions the people would. State facts that even Trump's most loyal supporters accept. Work your strength—the truth. I like it when I can't tell what the reporter thinks of this president. A great example is Lesley Stahl of *60 Minutes*...The key is to be professional, the more formal the better. If Trump gets publicly angry and aggressive, that's the most important time to act most professional."

Matthews's NBC colleague, Andrea Mitchell, agrees. "I don't want this to be an adversarial position. I think there's a healthy give-and-take with presidents, with politicians of all stripes. I've covered Democratic presidents and Republican presidents and I'm always sort of the loudmouth asking questions, shouting questions at Reagan...The designated shouter, you know, yelling questions when he went to and from the helicopter. And so they would give him a picture book with photos of the correspondents and we would be arrayed...the crazies...the mainstream media...and the friendly... And they would tell him...if you really want to get the American people to sympathize with you, call on the shouters, the real crazy ones...And, you know, when Donald Trump calls on Jim Acosta, he's trying to set up that context."[60]

Acosta gets the message. An administration insider actually told him his nickname is "Public Enemy Number One." On an average day Acosta is tough, but he was determined to stand his ground at a post-midterm-election press conference in November 2018. As White House correspondents shot questions at the president, Acosta asked his over and over, refusing to relinquish the microphone until he got an answer. You could look at his behavior two ways—tenacious reporting or really bad form. "So, call me a showboater or a grandstander or 'fake news.' I will go to my grave convinced deep down in my bones that journalists are performing a public service for the good of the country. The country is better off with reporters in the White House Briefing Room asking hard questions, even if we sometimes sound a little over-the-top. That noise is the sound that a healthy, functioning democracy makes."[61]

White House Press Secretary Sarah Sanders fired back at Acosta. "The White House cannot run an orderly and fair press conference when a reporter acts this way, which is neither appropriate nor professional...He refused to surrender a White House microphone to an intern so that other reporters might ask their questions."[62]

For liberal political junkies, Jim Acosta may qualify as the Dan Rather of his generation, taking on Trump the way Rather confronted Richard Nixon. Republican critics voice equally strong condemnation, calling Acosta disrespectful and disruptive. This particular news conference degenerated into a food fight. Trump accused Acosta of being "a rude, terrible person," and journalists quickly took sides. Many defended their colleague, but Chris Wallace, the host of *FOX News Sunday* and one of the coolest heads at the conservative network, called Acosta "a showboat...and that makes it awfully hard to have journalistic solidarity...I think he embarrassed himself...First of all, it was more of an argument than a question.

He was disrespectful to his colleagues in asking repeated questions and, thereby, making it harder for them to get in a question. Then the president of the United States told him to sit down, and he refused, and he kept talking."63

White House reaction was swift and harsh. They pulled Acosta's press credential, his White House hard pass, effectively freezing him out and compromising his ability to do his job. CNN filed a lawsuit citing the First Amendment and issued this statement: "While the suit is specific to CNN and Acosta, this could have happened to anyone...If left unchallenged, the actions of the White House would create a dangerous chilling effect for any journalist who covers elected officials."64 In this battle, there were strange allies and strange enemies. FOX News stood in solidarity with the Washington press corps, backing rival CNN and the outspoken Acosta. Jay Wallace, the president of FOX News, issued this statement: "While we don't condone the growing antagonistic tone by both the president and the press at recent media avails, we do support a free press, access, and open exchanges for the American people."65 Taking that stand, FOX News found itself pitted against White House Deputy Chief of Staff for Communications Bill Shine, a former high-ranking FOX executive with deep roots and enduring friendships at the network. It was an unlikely combination of strange bedfellows and strange "frenemies."

Plenty was written about the Acosta–Trump faceoff. Margaret Sullivan urged CNN to sue in an effort to restore Acosta's credential. She later told me, "I think Jim Acosta is a tough and smart journalist who also sometimes veers into grandstanding by calling attention to himself, not knowing when to take a step backwards. It might not be everyone's favorite style, but I think it is within the bounds of legitimate journalism...If the president or government officials can pick and choose who covers them, the whole concept of a free and independent press goes away and we're into autocratic territory that is really oppositional to what America stands for and what our Constitution says."

When the dialogue gets really ugly, both sides lose to some degree. Andrea Mitchell believes Donald Trump enjoys bantering with the press. "He calls us 'the enemy of the people.' He's branded us this way and it's taken. And it has diminished not only the power and authority but the credibility of the news media. And, I think, in a very damaging way."[66]

Former *60 Minutes* correspondent Lara Logan agrees. "I have profound respect for my colleagues and for what journalists are at our best. Today, as a whole, we are not at our best. Just ask people in towns and cities across the country, as I do. Everywhere I go, people tell me they have lost faith in journalism. It comes from all people. All walks of life and all political stripes."[67]

So what is the proper and most effective response from journalists? Margaret Sullivan echoes the sentiments of her *Washington Post* boss, Executive Editor Marty Baron. "We're not at war. We're at work. And his concept is simply keep our heads down, stay out of the fray, and do the best possible journalism and let that speak for us. Now, Marty, at the same time, is a staunch defender of a free press, and if one of the *Post* reporters had his or her press credential revoked, I am sure there would be some sort of action. But I don't think we want to accept the idea that we are at war with the president. I think that is absolutely detrimental. If he wants to present it that way, he can. That is his right of free speech and he can use the office as he sees fit. But we don't have to accept those terms."

David Gergen is one of the most respected and experienced political analysts. He had key roles in four administrations—Nixon,

Ford, Reagan, and Clinton. Later, he was founding director of the Center for Public Leadership at the Harvard Kennedy School. In addition, he's a senior political analyst for CNN and one of the most perceptive observers of the body politic. Gergen sees danger on the horizon and believes Donald Trump's attacks on the press could have devastating consequences. History tells us two ways to foster dictatorships are to spread disinformation and to silence the press. Gergen sees "trend lines now in this country that are a presage to authoritarianism...We are not there yet, but we should be very vigilant. We should be afraid. Very afraid."[68]

Frank Sesno, an award-winning journalist with more than thirty years of experience, is another Washington insider who spent twenty-one years as a CNN correspondent, anchor, and Washington Bureau Chief. He covered five presidents during a contentious but relatively civilized era. Sesno told me, "I've never seen anything like this. I've never seen a president who so routinely, deliberately, and maliciously attacks the institutions at the core of American democracy, the press included. There's plenty to criticize about the American media—always has been. Ask Thomas Jefferson, FDR, Ronald Reagan. They all had arguments about coverage that they felt was over-the-top, unfair, irresponsible, sensational, even dangerous. They made their feelings known, but they never went after individuals and institutions in such a ruinous way. I would describe the current conditions as perilously corrosive. They generate false impressions and false enemies. They magnify the already polarized politics that afflict the country at this time. Through constant attack, denial of fact, and use of consistently false narratives, the president undermines public confidence in journalism, in evidence-based reporting, and in my view, in the presidency itself as a bully pulpit that should be respected by all Americans. Some media outlets, by constantly focusing on the president's statements and misstatements and his tweets and attacks, play into the president's assertion that the press is not merely an adversary but an enemy. But the media are not the enemy. They are influential arbiters of information and public discourse. They can be annoying, even irresponsible. But they hold the president—and all in power—to account. They should do it consistently, respectfully, and carefully so that the public has confidence in the process and the profession of journalism." As director of the School of Media and Public Affairs at George Washington University, Sesno is imparting that wisdom to the journalists of tomorrow who may never deal directly with Donald Trump, but will face new challenges and benefit from the collective wisdom of hindsight.

To get a clear picture of what's happening, just survey the cable landscape. Flip from FOX to CNN to MSNBC. The differences are not subtle. They're stunning. Margaret Sullivan says, "I wouldn't make a real equation between what FOX News does and what the other cable networks do or what NBC or CBS or ABC do because, for the most part, those other organizations are essentially trying to report the news. Yes, they may come at it from a particular perspective, some more than others, but they are adhering to reality for the most part. FOX News doesn't always do that. And when they don't do it, they're not very good at correcting themselves or fessing up. So I think they're in a separate category that is, in my mind, problematic. Now, that doesn't mean they don't have solid, good journalists working there. They clearly do. But there is a mentality that is very close to verging on propaganda at times. Pro-Trump propaganda."

Margaret Sullivan thinks Bret Baier is fair and balanced. Chris Matthews agrees. He also praises "Chris Wallace and Shepard Smith...George F. Will, Maureen Dowd, the reporters at the *The Washington Post* and *The New York Times*."

In the past, every president had media adversaries and fought them using clandestine tactics—complaining to editors, limiting access, playing favorites, and giving exclusives to the competition. Reporters expected those lines of attack and sometimes wore presidential criticism as a badge of honor, especially if they made Richard Nixon's infamous "Enemies List" during the Vietnam War. Nixon believed the press "kicked him around" and relished turning the tables when he occupied the seat of power. Comparing the Trump era with previous administrations, Chris Matthews draws a crucial distinction. "Richard Nixon said that 'the press is the enemy.' He meant they were HIS enemies. That's certainly how he saw it. To say reporters are 'enemies of the people' is simply Trump's way of positioning himself as the people's tribune...I've noticed that the president mainly attacks the front page and network news reporters. He spends little time with the commentators and opinion press."

To complicate matters, overzealous Trump supporters threaten the press and commit violence possibly empowered by hateful diatribes from a leader who should know better. Frank Sesno believes the atmosphere is toxic. "And it is dangerous. Someone is going to hurt, if they haven't already, as a result of this. Though the media share responsibility, setting the tone of public debate—as do politicians and other public figures—it is the president who leads. He has Teddy Roosevelt's bully pulpit. He should be a role model. President Trump does not see the value in a free press, or the critical eye of independent journalism that is, yes, annoying and always critical, but also a cornerstone of the ribald give-and-take that defines us as a culture...If the public believes that holding the powerful to account is somehow treasonous, that it represents the actions of 'enemies of the people,' we threaten lives, journalism, and our premise that our democracy should be open, vibrant, and beholden to the people. Again, this doesn't excuse journalistic excess, shortcomings, ratings-driven decision making, sensationalism, bias, or any of the real-world criticisms and challenges that journalism confronts. But there is a very big difference between criticizing outcomes and attacking motivations. I know of no one in the media who is 'an enemy of the people.' Far from it. Most journalists—those who are professional, responsible, and real—consider themselves champions of the public and strive to convey the stories that affect the lives, pocketbooks, and futures of their audience."

That's the mission of Big J Journalism, but in this climate, speaking truth to power is a dangerous occupation. Some outspoken reporters are walking around with targets on their backs. As verbal animosity escalates, so does physical danger, prompting networks and newspapers to beef up security that proved essential on October 24, 2018 when a pipe bomb was delivered to CNN headquarters at the Time Warner Center in the heart of New York City. Anchors Jim Sciutto and Poppy Harlow were forced to evacuate during a live newscast as alarms blared in the background. In a coordinated attack, prominent Democrats were also targeted. It was a moment that crystalized the depth of the battle and its potential danger. Jim Acosta wrote, "This was a terrorist attack on my news organization and, without a doubt, the American free press...It had been building to some kind of act of violence...I feared the day would come when the president's rhetoric would lead one of his supporters to harm or even murder a journalist. And when it happened, the United States would undergo something of a sea change, joining a list of countries around the world where journalists were no longer safe reporting the truth."[69]

And how did our president react that October day when pipe bombs were also sent to the Clintons and Obamas? Donald Trump refused to mention CNN by name and referred to our ex-presidents as generic "former high-ranking officials." He never uttered the words "assassination attempts against two former presidents and a major news network." He called the pipe bombs "suspicious devices" not "lethal weapons," diluting the gravity of attacks that might have killed rival titans in the opposition party and the media.

That night, President Trump uttered bland, scripted comments at a political rally in Wisconsin where he blamed the victims. What a missed opportunity to be presidential. What a missed opportunity to be a moral leader. Conservative Bill Kristol suggested Trump should have "invited the Clintons and the Obamas to the White House"[70] in a show of respect and unity. Instead he whitewashed the facts.

Mika Brzezinski, cohost of MSNBC's *Morning Joe*, was quick to label Donald Trump's lukewarm statement "a low point in a presidency filled with lows."[71] The president's response, or lack thereof, accentuated the chasm between "Teleprompter Trump," when his staff is in momentary control, and "Twitter Trump," when he rants off script. His vicious tweet storms and ad libs raise troubling questions. If we hold ISIS leadership responsible when a lone wolf is "ISIS-inspired," is it legitimate to hold the president responsible when a lone wolf is "Trump-inspired"? Margaret Sullivan thinks that "The president's rhetoric does create an atmosphere that is potentially dangerous. But I hesitate to draw a direct connection. I don't think there is a direct connection. I do think if you have someone who's mentally unstable and has been thinking about doing something and you've got the president harshly criticizing different groups or individual people, it could tip over into violence. That's very worrisome. Words do matter and the president's words matter a great deal."

Thankfully, we're not living in a hot war zone, but our national dialogue has degenerated into a verbal cold war and the time bomb is ticking. Journalist Matthew Continetti believes Donald Trump did not cause the ugly divisions in our country. He believes volatile tensions predated Trump's ride down the escalator. His theory is that the would-be president sensed the divide and exploited it, "ripping thin skin off" and exposing raw nerve endings. Others argue Donald Trump was no more responsible than Bernie Sanders when one of his supporters shot and critically wounded Representative Steve Scalise and four others at a GOP softball practice in Washington. In the aftermath, there was one big difference. Sanders and other Democrats condemned the shooter and never tried to whitewash or diminish the severity of the attack.

There was a polar opposite reaction from far-right media titans when the CNN pipe bomber struck. They denied facts and distorted truth. Conservative grand dame Ann Coulter called the attacks a "false flag" crafted by Democrats as an "October surprise" ahead of the midterm elections. Conservative kingpin Rush Limbaugh didn't think the story passed the "smell test" and agreed with Coulter's October surprise theory. He floated the idea that since none of the bombs exploded, the whole episode was a setup to make the president and his followers look guilty. Another conservative stalwart, Laura Ingraham, hosted a panel of law enforcement experts on her primetime program on FOX. They claimed the bombs were harmless "theater" and the bomber was just "sending a message." Twenty-four hours later, the FBI arrested Cesar Sayoc, the alleged bomber. His explosives were rudimentary but could have injured intended targets and innocent bystanders. Sayoc was later indicted by the feds in the Southern District of New York on thirty felony counts and faces life in prison. Sounds more like true crime than harmless theater.

As the Trump v. Media battle morphed into all-out war, the rules of engagement were reinterpreted. Many journalists openly took sides. Ironically, the prescient line from *Network* captured the moment. The media was "mad as hell and not going to take it anymore." As the dialogue escalated, David Gergen cautioned the media to be prudent, saying, "There's a difference between a watchdog and a Rottweiler." And Frank Sesno believes, "There are some journalists who protest too much, who live off their Trumpian outrage and portray more offense than is productive. Journalists are judged too. They should cover the story, not BE the story."

Former CBS Anchor Scott Pelley wrote, "When reporters make every story essentially about themselves, we squander the public trust. We undermine the indispensable role of journalism in democracy. This is no small thing. Cynicism, as distinct from healthy skepticism, allowed President Trump to describe the media as 'a great danger' to our country...Mr. Trump attacked *CBS Evening News* as an 'enemy of the American people.' Days later, at the White House, I suggested to Mr. Trump that his 'enemy of the American people' language could lead some deranged soul to commit violence...I asked him to consider the consequences. He thought for a moment and said, 'I don't worry about that.'"[72]

Covering this story is especially complex for conservative reporters who adhere to right-wing policies but disavow Donald Trump's venom. Matthew Lewis is a columnist at *The Daily Beast* and a CNN contributor. He said, "President Trump declared war on the media and now the media has declared war on Trump." Lewis says since he's part of the media, it makes it difficult for him to express his conservative viewpoints and simultaneously defend his profession.

Margaret Sullivan watches hours of television news as media columnist at *The Washington Post*. She covers right, left, and center programming. "Our country is very split, a divided populace. And people want to see their point of view affirmed. However, I think we can hold people to the standard of fairness and truthfulness. They may not be completely neutral. Is Rachel Maddow completely neutral? No. She certainly has a political leaning that shines through. But is she fair and is she truthful? I think more so than Sean Hannity, yes."

One night, Maddow claimed to have an exclusive look at Donald Trump's tax returns. As a producer who worked in television news for decades, I notice production values. Try watching Rachel Maddow with a stopwatch. At the top of the broadcast, there's virtually no videotape and very few graphics. It's all Rachel all the time. Her opening monologue can run twenty minutes. That's not an introduction. It's a lecture.

"It is a speech," Margaret Sullivan agrees. When Maddow "gained access to this report about his tax returns and it was touted as this huge breaking news thing, she spent a long lead-up that really didn't say much. And it was very frustrating from the viewer's point of view and I think it was not the best practice. That's a hallmark of Rachel Maddow's and some people like it. They feel as though she's explaining the news to them and explaining the context. In a sense, it's refreshing because we're in a nanosecond response cycle. So, in a way, it's nice to have someone take a little bit more time."

Loyal viewers of *The Rachel Maddow Show* are not deterred by her signature lengthy monologues. But, in my view, her best moments happen when she lands the "big get." Case in point, her Lev Parnas exclusive in January 2020. The Trump associate was a shadowy figure until Maddow thrust him into the spotlight. Parnas appeared to be well coached and well prepared. But Maddow was on her game, asking clear and concise questions, drawing out new information the way a skilled prosecutor lays out the timeline of a case. It was informational, not confrontational.

When reporters operate in a verbal combat zone, some may be tempted to lose their cool. But in the age of Trump, when female minority reporters were repeatedly singled out for criticism, they maintained their dignity and principles. President Trump accused Yamiche Alcindor of asking "a racist question" when she asked whether his rhetoric emboldens white nationalists. Alcindor is the White House Correspondent for the PBS *News Hour* and previously worked for the *New York Times*. During the coronavirus epidemic, the president intensified his attacks, repeatedly insulting her questions that pointed out contradictions between Trump's previous statements and what actually happened. The contempt he unleashed on Alcindor was unwarranted and tinged with racism.

The president also demeaned Abby Phillip of CNN for asking "a lot of stupid questions." Phillip has twenty-four karat credentials. Prior to joining CNN, she graduated from Harvard and worked for *The Washington Post*.

But perhaps his favorite female target was April Ryan, White House Correspondent for American Urban Radio. The president called her "a loser...who doesn't know what she's doing." Ryan fought back, maintaining grace under pressure but sending a very strong message. She said the Trump White House is "putting a target on our heads because we are asking questions maybe they don't like...For the last twenty years I've been doing this.

I've asked the same kinds of questions, literally of Bill Clinton, of George W. Bush, of Barack Obama, and now this president. The only question I never asked those presidents that I asked this president was 'Mr. President, are you a racist?'"[73] Ryan's tenacity did not go unnoticed by white supremacists. Her life was threatened in vile racial tirades.

Media colleagues rallied to defend minority reporters chastised by the president. Jim Acosta said, "To April, I became her 'brother from another mother.' April was my 'sister from another mister.' She and I had something else in common: we were both receiving death threats, and at levels we had not experienced before. April would later confide in me that she had the FBI on speed dial."[74]

"The president has a tendency to go after particular subsets of people," Margaret Sullivan told me. "He's been particularly critical of journalists of color. That was true during the campaign and it remained true. So I don't think it's a coincidence that he has gone after, very harshly, three black women journalists. That's not a coincidence. It's a pattern."

Most of the venom directed at the press did not have a racial component. Jim Acosta received Twitter messages threatening gruesome, medieval torture. Brian Stelter, host of CNN's *Reliable Sources*, was repeatedly threatened. On the campaign trial, young female correspondents were menaced at Trump rallies. MSNBC's Katy Tur received a terrifying note: "I hope you get raped and killed." It was signed MAGA. At a televised rally, Tur was singled out by the president. "These people back here, they're the worst. They are so dishonest. She's back there, little Katy. She's back there." Looking back, Tur wrote, "Imagine someone calling you a liar. Now amplify the experience by a thousand if a presidential candidate calls you a liar. And tack on another factor of ten if that presidential candidate is named Donald J. Trump. Waves of insults and threats poured into my phone—the device buzzing like a shock collar."[75]

At one point, things got so contentious Trump refused to appear on NBC until Tur apologized for what he perceived as negative coverage. "Apparently tweeting that I should be fired, calling me a liar in front of millions of people on national television, and receiving death threats from his followers shortly thereafter was not enough punishment. He wants penance. He wants groveling. He wants to hear those two precious words. And until he gets them, he says no *NBC Nightly News*. No *Meet the Press*. No *Today Show*."[76] A week later, Katy Tur did apologize—to the executive producer of *Today* because Trump was boycotting them in favor of archrival ABC's *Good Morning America*. Eventually, the storm subsided, but the animosity remained. Trump supporters continued their harassment of Tur, her network, and her family, prompting NBC to hire security guards to protect her during events and escort her to her car after filing the last report. On election night, Katy Tur was told by a Trump staffer that except for the president, "You're the most-watched person in the room. The Secret Service has eyes on you."[77] Is that supposed to be reassuring or terrifying?

Television reporters weren't the only targets. The potential for violence loomed ominously across the broad spectrum of political journalism. *New York Times* reporter Ken Vogel received a threatening voicemail saying, "You are the problem. You are the enemy of the people. The pen may be mightier than the sword. The pen is not mightier than the AK-47."[78] And a California Trump supporter was arrested for threatening to shoot up the *Boston Globe* newsroom, echoing the president's mantra "fake news." These were not isolated incidents. Death threats and intimidation reached unprecedented levels as the White House and the free press battled it out. CNN analyst David Gergen offered a sobering comparison: "Donald Trump has outpaced Richard Nixon in disparaging the press."[79]

Reflecting on Trump's anti-press tirades, is there a method to his madness? Is there a direct correlation between his anti-press invectives and his approval ratings? At various times, the numbers seem to indicate there is a correlation. As Chris Matthews observed, "I think the press-bashing and the job approval move in tandem." But Frank Senso looks at different numbers at different time periods and disagrees. "His ratings really don't move. In fact, I think the more he beats up the press, the more he hurts himself in the long run. Harry Truman famously said, 'The buck stops here.' Trump is always passing the buck. He accepts responsibility for nothing. Blaming the press may please his base and amuse those who think the media are irresponsible and worse, but this approach will not hold up to the scrutiny of time and experience. Most Americans disapprove of the president's performance. And most distrust the media."

Midway through the Trump presidency, Republicans and Democrats faced off in crucial midterm elections. The tone was set at the top and the tone was brutal. President Trump spent enormous amounts of time at political rallies, reinforcing the belief that he prefers barnstorming to governing.

On the campaign trail, Donald Trump's number-one political target was his immediate predecessor, Barack Obama. Historians will document that battle of titans in copious detail. Who succeeded and who failed? One barometer will be their handling of the economy. Remember James Carville's bumper sticker "It's the economy, stupid." That prompts the question: how did the press cover economic issues?

Financial journalist Consuelo Mack is the anchor of *Wealthtrack with Consuelo Mack* on PBS. She points out, "Financial coverage by general and political reporters on national and local news television is basically nonexistent. It doesn't get assigned or reported because it doesn't get ratings unless there's a scandal involved, or visual layoffs, labor unrest, or if the market does something dramatic over several days either up or down. When financial trends do get reported, they frequently don't make air. Most general news and political reporters have not studied the economy and markets. It's considered a journalistic niche with little currency:"

In addition to the paucity and superficiality of coverage, Mack told me journalists may not be neutral. "For starters, numerous surveys have found that as a group, print journalists are overwhelmingly liberal. Ninety percent identified themselves as either Democrats or Independents. Only seven percent said they were Republicans. I don't know about TV reporters per se, but I would be surprised if they were significantly different. That doesn't mean they cannot be objective…Historically, mainstream TV programs like *60 Minutes* have a reputation for being antibusiness and liberal. Such is not the case on the business news networks…Stuart Varney and Trish Reagan on FOX Business are known to be pro-free market and in some cases pro-Trump. Joe Kernen on CNBC expresses similar sentiments."

During the 2018 midterms, President Trump could have accentuated the positive by touting the booming economy as the cornerstone of his message. But he opted to go negative. Forget the economy card. He played the immigration card, dwelling on migrant caravans approaching our southern border. He labeled indigent mothers and children "ISIS terrorists and MS-13 gang members." In a calculated show of force, he dispatched approximately 5,600 military troops to the Texas border. Reacting to the troop movements, media critics were quick to point out a pattern. Donald

Trump acts like a bully when he's confronting the vulnerable, but he's weak when confronting powerful titans like Vladimir Putin and Kim Jong-un.

As the caravan approached, some television channels took the bait and focused on the border standoff. Others, as Frank Sesno told me, took a broader, more informative view. "In the midst of the caravan traveling up through Mexico, there were repeated tweet storms from the president. But some news organizations pursued coverage that sought to explain who these people were, where they came from, and how sanctuary and asylum worked."

By the time Election Day arrived on November 6, the knives were sufficiently sharpened and both political parties were ready for the kill. Off-year elections are traditionally referendums on the president, and this was no exception. The name Donald J. Trump was not on the ballot, but metaphorically it was flashing neon ten feet tall. And to make sure Trump voters were sufficiently pumped, on election eve the president headlined a rally in Missouri to support Republican senatorial candidate Josh Hawley, who was poised to unseat Democrat Claire McCaskill. Donald Trump was the star attraction, surrounded by a supporting cast of media titans. Sean Hannity and Jeanine Pirro joined him on the podium and gave brief speeches endorsing the president's values. Hannity and Pirro were not "reporting." They were "campaigning." Hannity gratuitously slammed the media, pointing at the working press: "All those people in the back are fake news." That apparently included his colleagues from FOX. This attack crossed a line and appalled some executives at the FOX mother ship in Manhattan.

After the rally, FOX management went into damage-control mode, issuing a statement: "FOX News does not condone any talent participating in campaign events...This was an unfortunate distraction and has been addressed."[80] Fast-forward twenty-four hours and Sean Hannity was MIA at FOX election central. He was scheduled to appear on set to analyze returns, but instead he was sidelined. No explanation was given, but his absence spoke volumes.

Media critic Margaret Sullivan reacted by saying, "When Sean Hannity is allowed to continue working at FOX News without any apparent major reprimand after going onstage with President Trump at a rally, we're into some whole new territory for a place that calls itself a news outlet...To me, some of the most problematic people on television are Sean Hannity, Tucker Carlson, and Laura Ingraham, who all have important slots...and to varying degrees, big ratings. They seem to be almost invulnerable at their network and I think they do harm."

The Hannity episode did not sit well with many reporters who struggle to keep their jobs and their personal politics in separate compartments. Chris Matthews recalled when his wife Kathleen ran for Congress in 2016, "I could not so much as knock on a door. I would have loved to go up and down every block telling everyone how much I admired her and supported her. My profession prevented it." Matthews adhered to the fundamental commandments of journalism. Hannity and Pirro did not.

As the midterm votes were tallied, Brit Hume at FOX predicted the Democrats' win in the House of Representatives would receive "adoring coverage from the media." He was right. The liberal spin machine hyped the House victory, while conservatives were gleeful about the GOP Senate win. Was this a case of two wrongs balancing out the coverage? Or were both sides wrong to appear partisan?

The morning after an election is traditionally a time to celebrate victory or mourn defeat. Nerves are frayed, and both sides need a time-out to regroup and plan ahead. But in 2018, calm was not on the horizon. Let the games resume and resume they did. Given a golden opportunity to act presidential, Donald Trump couldn't stay above the fray. He was incapable of being gracious and used the moment to settle scores with rival politicians and the working press. Margaret Sullivan makes the observation, "It really benefits President Trump with his base to be harshly criticizing journalists because it's this group of coastal people from New York and Washington. Trump is telling his base 'I understand you. We sort of hate the same people.'"

As the election results drifted into the netherworld of yesterday's news, the Mueller investigation dominated the headlines. In any battle, peripheral titans are often thrust into the conflict. They can fuel the fire or calm things down. Compare the dynamics during the Clinton impeachment and the Muller investigation. Both confrontations had bitter partisan overtones, but during the Clinton probe, Independent Counsel Kenneth Starr never met a microphone he didn't like. He was here, there, and everywhere prejudging Bill Clinton. In contrast, during the Trump investigation, Special Counsel Robert Muller was the quintessential quiet man refusing to litigate his case in the glare of the spotlight. As the Mueller investigation dragged on, Trump's war on the press accelerated, with FOX protecting him on the right flank and CNN and MSNBC returning fire on the left.

Media insiders on all sides of the political spectrum are trying to determine the impact this ongoing battle of titans will have on the future of journalism. In the short term, cable news networks are making money. Ratings are up and controversy is proving beneficial for the bottom line. Jill Lepore of *The New Yorker* thinks that "Scrutiny of the administration has produced excellent work, the very best of journalism...Trump is the Nixon to today's rising generation of Woodwards and Bernsteins. Superb investigative reporting is published every day by news organizations both old and new...By the 'what doesn't kill you' line of argument, the more forcefully Trump attacks the press, the stronger the press becomes. Unfortunately, that's not the full story."[81]

One casualty of the battle is Trump fatigue. Kyle Pope of the *Columbia Journalism Review* thinks, "Behind the drop-off in quality is burnout, both among readers and reporters tasked with doing the dance. The burnout stems both from the sheer number of hours worked, and also from the fact that a lot of the early investigative works seems to have had so little impact. Journalists aren't supposed to pay attention to the effect of their stories—do the piece and let the chips fall—but we're all human and a certain demoralization has sunk in. Despite everything we've learned about Trump over the year, the size of his core support hasn't budged. If anything, they've doubled down on their support of the president, almost because of the journalistic attacks."[82]

Jeffrey Toobin of CNN sees one bright spot. In a recent interview, he told this journalist that in unexpected ways, "Trump's presidency has been a good period for journalism. There has been a lot of excellent coverage of him. We are responsible for telling the truth. We are not responsible for persuading people to reject or embrace a politician...Just tell the truth. If we are accurate and fair, it doesn't matter if we are criticized for being biased, in my opinion."

While Donald Trump was busy bashing the press, he found plenty of time to bash his Democratic rivals and dissident Republicans. Simultaneously, a few journalists found time to attack each other. One high-profile battle pitted Ted Koppel against Sean Hannity in a revealing exchange that was part generational, part ideological. In a televised interview, Hannity responded to Koppel's question by posing one of his own. "Do you really think I'm bad for America?" Koppel didn't skip a beat. "Yes, I do."[83] It was a dramatic faceoff between two media titans who are diametrically opposed. Koppel is a decades-long purist in the annals of journalism history. Hannity insists he's not even a reporter. He just plays one on TV. Commenting later, Koppel elaborated, clarifying what he meant. "I thought he was bad for America because there is a tendency on programs like his, and I made the point that it was also true of programs on the left as well as programs on the right, of people favoring ideology over facts. That is what I think is bad for America."[84]

Koppel lobbed criticism at two other television hosts, Al Sharpton and Lou Dobbs. "Listen, I had a conversation with the then president of NBC News a long time ago [about Sharpton] and I said, 'How can you allow a guy to have what masquerades as some kind of a news program who then leaves the studio and goes off and leads a rally?...It's an inappropriate activity."[85]

Regarding Lou Dobbs and his cozy relationship with Donald Trump, Koppel said, "Is it appropriate? No! It's not appropriate... [and] things can be perceived as negative about what our friends at CNN and MSNBC are doing. Don't misunderstand. Yes, I am outraged by what appears on FOX. But that doesn't make me any happier to see MSNBC moving further and further in that direction."[86]

Some media giants are over-the-top partisans, while others may have subliminal conflicts because they've worked both sides of the street—launching their careers as political operatives before switching to journalism. Former *Hardball* host Chris Matthews was a speechwriter for Jimmy Carter and chief of staff for powerful Democratic Speaker of the House Tip O'Neill. "A solid advantage, having worked in politics for so many years," says Matthews, "is that

I know what partisan arguments sound like…I learned to see things from the inside."

Lawrence O'Donnell, also of MSNBC, was a political aide to Democratic senator Daniel Patrick Moynihan, and his colleague Joe Scarborough made his bones as a GOP congressman from the Florida Panhandle. At FOX, Dana Perino was press secretary for President George W. Bush. CNN anchor Chris Cuomo never worked in politics, but picked up insights by osmosis. His father Mario and brother Andrew both served as governors of New York State. And of course, George Stephanopoulos at ABC and the late Tim Russert of NBC conquered the worlds of politics and journalism with exceptional skill. Being a political insider can be polarizing or it can be a powerful asset when reporting from outside the tent. Knowing the players and knowing how they think takes some of the mystery out of reporting.

Multiple factors are at play, overshadowing the day-of-air craziness that leaves little time for serious reflection. Dealing with the Trump administration, television journalists are exploring options while battling an existential threat from the president of the United States. Let's not underestimate him. Donald Trump is a formidable adversary who was reinvigorated after avoiding removal from office in a historic Senate vote. Immediately after the Senate gave him a free pass, Trump reverted to campaign mode and bashed the press even harder.

To survive these unrelenting attacks, journalists under fire must sublimate professional rivalries and present a united front. An attack on one is an attack on all. The challenge is to respond as quickly, effectively and fairly as possible. It's probably too soon to tell who's winning this battle of titans and who's losing. There will be plenty of postwar analysis. We call it "history" and it hasn't been written yet.

CHAPTER THREE

FROM JUST THE FACTS TO OUTRAGEOUS OPINIONS

It was a defining moment in the history of broadcast journalism when America's most revered anchorman, Walter Cronkite, rendered his verdict on the controversial Vietnam War. "We'd like to sum up our findings in Vietnam...Who won or lost the great Tet Offensive against the cities? I'm not sure. The Vietcong did not win by a knockout, but neither did we...It seems more certain than ever that the bloody experience of Vietnam is to end in a stalemate...It is increasingly clear to this reporter that the only rational way out then will be to negotiate."[87]

This statement may seem tame compared to the inflammatory rhetoric we hear today, but in February 1968 it was revolutionary. Walter Cronkite was the voice of reasoned objectivity in a tumultuous era. But, at that moment, he wasn't just delivering facts. He was expressing an opinion. Cronkite weighed the options and made a calculated choice to cross the Rubicon and deliver his message directly to the American people and the American president. To many, it was an inevitable reflection of the headlines he was reporting. Antiwar students were burning draft cards as flag-draped coffins made somber journeys to cemeteries across America. Generations were pitted against each other here at home, and over a million people were dying halfway around the world.

According to Joel Achenbach of *The Washington Post*, "A Cronkite moment is no longer possible because the news ecosystem today is too fragmented. Many Americans would be hard-pressed to name the current anchor of *The CBS Evening News*. Cronkite's great persuasive power emerged from his long history of not attempting to be persuasive at all. That allowed him to fly to Vietnam like an intercontinental ballistic missile of objectivity. But the past half century has seen a steady erosion in the trust Americans place in institutions such as news media. Partisan journalists, wielding verbal flamethrowers, view their objective counterparts as retailers of false balance. The media culture no longer requires or wants someone with the authority of Cronkite to say, as he did every night at the close of his broadcast, 'And that's the way it is'...Today, Cronkite's daring, historic, precedent-busting words about Vietnam would probably be greeted with hot takes of outrage, for one reason or another—in the brief moment before those words were lost in the noise."[88]

While politicians were eager to voice their positions for or against the Vietnam War, anchormen exercised restraint. There were subtle innuendos—an arched eyebrow here or a pejorative adjective there—but you had to read between the lines. The only outright opinions were clearly labeled "commentary" and came near the end of the broadcast. Eric Sevareid appeared regularly on Walter Cronkite's program and fulfilled the role of eminence gris. Behind the scenes in the hallowed watering holes of Washington and New York, opinions were rampant. But once the red light appeared on the studio camera, there were strict rules of engagement and the Federal Communications Commission enforced them with the Fairness Doctrine and Equal Time regulations that governed broadcast news divisions. Ted Koppel recalls, "There was a time when the Federal Communications Commission, in effect, said to the commercial television networks, 'Look, we're letting you have a one-hundred-dollar bill printing press in your basements. You can make as much money as you want to make on *I Love Lucy* and *Gunsmoke* and *77 Sunset Strip*. But, in exchange for that, we expect that you will operate in the public interest, necessity, and convenience.' And what that meant was 'We expect you to have functioning news divisions that cover the important issues around the world.' Up until 1987, we had something called the Fairness Doctrine. The Fairness Doctrine was sort of a mushy, fuzzy piece of legalese but essentially it required that if networks put on someone in a debate with a liberal point of view, it had to be balanced by someone holding a conservative point of view. In 1987, the Fairness Doctrine was eliminated under the Reagan administration. And in 1988, a young man by the name of Rush Limbaugh began broadcasting because for the first time, this notion of maintaining fairness, balance, and objectivity was no longer required. And Rush was enormously successful and remained successful…As talk radio developed, the right found an audience and the left didn't. You know, it's always sort of been interesting to me that right-wing radio has flourished in this country. Left-wing efforts to do something similar have failed. But left-wing comedy, especially late-night comedy, has been a gigantic success. And much of what has flowed over the past thirty years since then has been an outgrowth of the elimination of the Fairness Doctrine."[89]

Noncompliance with the old FCC mandate could cost a television station its license. So when Walter Cronkite broke the gentlemen's agreement to conceal his personal feelings, it may not have been a surprise to his friends and colleagues or his most discerning viewers, yet it made headlines and possibly changed the course of history because the American public trusted "Uncle Walter." Kenneth T. Walsh noted, "It may be hard to believe in the current era of declining media credibility and amid President Donald Trump's bitter condemnations of 'fake news,' but mainstream journalists once were trusted figures in society who could sway public opinion in major way."[90]

The ripple effect of Cronkite's pronouncement rapidly morphed into a tsunami. A few weeks later on Sunday night March 31,1968, President Lyndon B. Johnson stunned the nation and the world with the words "I shall not seek, and I will not accept, the nomination of my party for another term as your president." Historical scholars agree the announcement was not forged in a vacuum. Johnson's withdrawal from the race was due in part to the Cronkite effect. LBJ reportedly lamented, "If I've lost Walter Cronkite, I've lost Middle America." Another key factor was the primary challenge led by Minnesota's Democratic Senator Eugene McCarthy. The erudite leader of the antiwar movement did not win the New Hampshire primary, but he received an impressive forty-two percent of the Democratic vote. That, coupled with the prospect of Bobby Kennedy waiting in the wings, sent a chill through the corridors of the Johnson White House.

Media watchdogs often debate the fine line between advocating for truth and advocating for policy. Throughout the annals of journalism, there were major turning points that illustrate the point. The Spanish–American War marked a turbulent era of "yellow journalism" spearheaded by newspaper magnate William Randolph Hearst.

Much later in the 1950s, a classic confrontation dominated small black-and-white television screens as CBS journalist Edward R. Murrow leveled attacks against Senator Joseph McCarthy, a Republican firebrand from Wisconsin. Murrow's broadcasts contributed to the downfall of the divisive senator who had co-opted the national stage and ruined lives by making baseless charges about alleged membership in the Communist party. Jack Mirkinson believes, "Murrow's attack on McCarthy has become legendary—an iconic example of journalistic guts…Murrow painted a picture of a man whose recklessness with the truth and ugly attacks on his critics contributed to a climate of deep fear and repression in American life."[91]

More than a decade passed before *New York* magazine hit the newsstands in 1968, ushering in "New Journalism," a reporting style heralded as a major innovation. It was an in-your-face approach that immersed the reporter in the story as more than just a neutral bystander. New Journalism was epitomized by talented and edgy writers including Tom Wolfe, Nick Pileggi, Gail Sheehy, Gloria Steinem, and Gay Talese. They selected controversial topics and voiced personal observations about the people and issues they were covering. Their hybrid style was widely praised for making stories come alive, and it was soundly criticized for injecting the writer's ego into the narrative. Michael J. Arlen wrote, "Journalism is perhaps in the kind of muddle it's in today not, Lord knows, because Tom Wolfe sat down at his bench one day and invented a new art form, but because people in general, editors as well as writers, as well as readers, have had trouble figuring out how to deal with this terrain…[In the past] the American press rested its weight upon the simple declarative sentence. The no-nonsense approach. Who? What? When? Just give us the facts, ma'am."[92]

As time passed, there were other watershed moments in political journalism. In the 1970s, it was Watergate. *The Washington Post* led the way with Pulitzer Prize–winning coverage by Bob Woodward and Carl Bernstein. On television screens, CBS was center stage with scathing reports from Dan Rather and Daniel Schorr, who earned a coveted spot on Richard Nixon's Enemies List.

After Nixon resigned, the political news front seemed to calm down. The public, politicians, and journalists all needed a breather—a time to heal. Headlines didn't seem as divisive as the focus shifted away from Vietnam and Watergate. It was an incubation period for seismic changes that were looming on the horizon. That happened on June 1, 1980 when Ted Turner's Cable News Network signed on with coverage twenty-four hours a day, seven days a week. Up to that point, ABC, CBS, and NBC had had a virtual monopoly with concise thirty-minute nightly newscasts.

"In its first years of operation, CNN lost money and was ridiculed as the Chicken Noodle Network…However, Turner continued to invest in building up the network's news bureaus…and CNN eventually came to be known for covering live events around the world as they happened."[93] Although news junkies can't imagine life without nonstop access, there were contemporaneous critics who debated the merits of wall-to-wall coverage, especially on slow news days when nothing much happens.

I remember a radio interview with David Brinkley, unconnected to the launch of CNN but nonetheless relevant. He was addressing the question of expanding nightly news from a succinct thirty minutes to one full hour. Brinkley was against it. He said most people think earth-shattering events happen every day in exotic foreign capitals around the globe. But in Brinkley's wry opinion, on an average day, nothing worth reporting happens in most major cities. In its infancy, CNN had to confront that problem. Some of their reports were repetitive, and some of their programs were loaded with time-killing features that qualified as filler, not news. Pundits still debate whether a twenty-four-hour news cycle is a necessary benefit or a necessary evil. On the upside, important events unfold unpredictably, so real-time coverage provides a window on the world for viewers who wish to monitor every twist and turn. Round-the-clock coverage is also a big plus for people with unorthodox schedules. If you work until midnight, you can return home to headlines and analysis.

While news coverage was always in a state of perpetual evolution, there was a watershed line of demarcation—a seminal moment when the evolution became a revolution. Enter Rupert Murdoch, Roger Ailes, and the FOX News Channel. It launched modestly on October 7, 1996 in seventeen million homes mostly in New York and Los Angeles. It was destined to become a behemoth, a game changer, as mainstream journalism drifted from just the facts to outrageous opinions.

Before we explore the impact of Murdoch and Ailes hijacking the news, a digression about the way things were before the tempo changed. From 1982–1988, I was a writer/producer at *WABC Eyewitness News* in New York City. During that period, we were often the top-rated newscast in the number-one market in the country. Our newsroom was populated by an eclectic cast of characters straight out of a movie—old newspaper guys, Upper West Side liberals, mensches, and sharks. Most of us were political junkies and had very strong opinions. But we checked our biases in the lobby, and by the time the elevator door opened on the newsroom floor, it was just the facts that mattered.

Behind the scenes in private conversations, Governor Mario Cuomo and Senator Bill Bradley were admired. Mayor Ed Koch was great copy because he was always camera ready with a punchy sound bite. Donald Trump and Reverend Al Sharpton were dismissed as headline-grabbing egotists—one a playboy, the other a demagogue. Think Tawana Brawley. While we didn't play partisan politics on the air, we lived and died by the ratings. Trump and Sharpton were the proverbial "train wreck" and reliably delivered eyeballs. They knew their power and used the press to boost their public profiles. In return, we used them to boost our ratings. Looking back, we owe our viewers a collective mea culpa. And we owe an even larger apology to the Central Park Five. It's disconcerting to realize two major events that defined the 1980s zeitgeist in New York City—Tawana Brawley's phony kidnapping and the rape of the Central Park Jogger—were not what they appeared at first glance. The police and the press got both stories terribly wrong.

Our primary anchor team during that era was the dynamic duo Roger Grimsby and Bill Beutel. Roger was the quintessential curmudgeon, a sardonic iconoclast. He didn't seem to like anybody or anything, so it was difficult for viewers to identify his ideological orientation. Bill Beutel concealed his political beliefs under the foreign correspondent's trench coat he wore so well. In many ways, the paring worked. Yin and yang.

In the 1990s, I was a senior producer at CNBC overseeing the launch of *Hardball with Chris Matthews*, Tim Russert's weekend interview program, and *The Dick Cavett Show*. Chris was a speechwriter at the Carter White House and later worked on Capitol Hill as chief of staff for Democratic Speaker of the House Tip O'Neill. Tim was a counselor for New York's Democratic governor, Mario Cuomo. Off the clock, both men had opinions. But on-air coverage really was "fair and balanced." We booked one guest from Column A and one from Column B—a liberal here, a conservative there. Moderators were impartial referees asking equally tough questions of both sides and letting the newsmakers battle it out.

In the early days of *Hardball*, some of our most popular guests used their appearances as springboards to become conservative superstars—Joe Scarborough, Kellyanne Conway, and Tucker Carlson. We gave them plenty of airtime to discuss the Clinton impeachment in all its lurid detail, and they did so with gusto. Their accusations were fair game because President Clinton was under active investigation by Independent Counsel Kenneth Starr and was subsequently impeached by the House of Representatives. Looking back to that era, a convincing case can be made that Speaker of the House Newt Gingrich effectively used television not only to batter Bill Clinton, but to create the toxic divide between red-state America and blue-state America that persists today. And we in the media unintentionally facilitated his crusade.

During my tenure at CNBC, there was rotating leadership in the executive suite. At one point, our president was Roger Ailes. I reported directly to one of his top lieutenants, the vice president of Primetime Programming, and had very little contact with Mr. Ailes. In all fairness, I must say Ailes never asked me to book or unbook a guest, to spike or plant a story. But behind the scenes, he was busy maneuvering, to the dismay of NBC brass headquartered at 30 Rock.

In 1996, Roger Ailes was forced out at CNBC and went full throttle when he launched FOX News Channel, the brainchild of

Australian media powerhouse Rupert Murdoch. Murdoch had already influenced news coverage in Australia and London and altered the face of American television by injecting tabloid production techniques, provocative banners, slow-motion shots, and dramatic reenactments of grisly crimes.

Murdoch's early television forays were entertainment oriented, not political. His new crown jewel, the FOX News Channel, would be all politics all the time, and despite the "fair and balanced" tagline, it would not pretend to be a neutral arbiter. The network was designed with a twofold objective—provide a platform for conservative policies and make money. Using those yardsticks, it was eminently successful. Right-wing pundits had already captured the talk radio market. Now they were branching out to the visual medium. FNC's formula was carefully calculated and inherently simple. It would be conservative talk radio with moving pictures.

Murdoch and Ailes changed the face of cable news and created powerful stars while masquerading as a legitimate news operation. But in reality, they were spreading the gospel according to the GOP. "There was no venue better equipped to reach Republican primary voters than FOX News. Its audience was comprised of the most passionate members of the conservative base. They provided votes, grassroots contributions, and boots on the ground. Winning the 'FOX primary' was perhaps as important as reaching voters in Iowa, New Hampshire, and South Carolina."[94]

Ted Koppel admits he watches FOX out of professional curiosity. "Well, I think first of all you have to acknowledge that [Ailes] and Murdoch showed a certain level of genius in perceiving that there was a significant portion of the American public that really was not happy with what they saw as being news that was skewed to the left of the political spectrum. Too liberal. So, they filled the need with FOX and filled it to such a degree that it became…hugely profitable…I think today they probably make somewhere in the neighborhood of two billion dollars a year."[95]

There was a perception that most journalists were secret lefties, and that enabled FOX to successfully fill a lucrative void. Toby Miller of the University of California sized it up this way: "CNN and FOX market themselves differently—the former to urban, highly educated viewers and the latter to rural, less-educated viewers. One functions like a broadsheet, the other like a tabloid, with CNN punditry coming mostly from outsiders, and FOX punditry as much from presenters as guests."[96]

If there was any doubt about bias, it was hard to miss when Barack Obama ascended to power. During the 2008 primaries, FOX News and real estate mogul Donald J. Trump collaborated to spread the "birther" myth. David Brock and Ari Rabin-Havt explored the phenomenon in their book *The FOX Effect*. "The facts did not matter. At FOX News, the start of the Obama presidency was about establishing a narrative that he was a weak, big-spending liberal who would ruin the country. By denying the president a honeymoon, Ailes set the tone for the rest of Obama's term. Instead of bringing America together, as Obama promised, FOX would work to ensure that we were torn apart."[97]

The attack sped into overdrive when President Obama proposed healthcare legislation. "Once again, FOX shed the pretense of objective journalism by repeatedly encouraging viewers to contact members of Congress to express their opposition to the bill. They slyly reported 'breaking news' that Rush Limbaugh was urging Americans to contact Congress and express their opposition to healthcare reform…Glenn Beck boosted Limbaugh's effort, saying 'Rush Limbaugh for only the second time in his career told his audience yesterday to flood the switchboards and, boy, did they ever. He's right. He said yesterday that this is the endgame. This is it. The fundamental transformation is here, America.'"[98]

Another FOX host, Mike Huckabee, told his audience, "Obama and House Speaker Nancy Pelosi are attempting to ram their massive healthcare bill through Congress...We must stop this bill. Huckabee urged those watching to 'call, email, write' to lawmakers and repeated his call to action while appearing on *Your World with Neil Cavuto*, aided by on-screen text reading 'Huckabee: Call Congress, Tell Them Vote No On Health Care.'"[99] What's wrong with this picture? Several things. News outlets are supposed to report the facts and let viewers make their own evaluations. Direct and impassioned "calls to action" are not the province of old-school journalism. Guests and pundits occasionally call to action, but party hacks impersonating TV journalists should not.

Supporters of FOX insist the daytime block is hard news while the primetime lineup is opinion just like the competition. But can the public really tell the difference? Sophisticated viewers may understand the distinction. But average viewers see a host wearing a suit, sitting behind an anchor desk, with "breaking news" banners scrolling as newsmakers discuss the day's events. It's a familiar formula that looks and sounds like a traditional newscast. Former FOX VP Bill Shine defended his network's approach and one of their most popular primetime hosts. "Sean [Hannity] is not a journalist. Sean is a conservative commentator. Sean doesn't hide, and never has hidden, his beliefs from anyone."[100]

Margaret Sullivan of *The Washington Post* thinks there should be a clear division of labor. Either you're a real journalist or a real partisan. "I don't think viewers make that distinction very well. We like to tell ourselves that they do, but in the old days when you read a print newspaper it was clear. There were news pages and then you got to the opinion pages, the editorial pages that were clearly marked, and everyone understood what it was. Now the way we receive information is in a disaggregated way, often coming to us on our phone. Every piece is sort of separate and we don't have that context. And that is true on television cable news. It's interesting to me to see FOX is using an advertising slogan 'Real News. Real Honest Opinion.' So they're clearly trying to draw the distinction that Sean Hannity is one thing and Bret Baier is quite another. And I agree with that. But I'm not sure viewers make that distinction very well."

In my view, perhaps we all need an attitude adjustment—a re-definition of terms. Some coverage is clearly not "news." Maybe hard news has been replaced by "talk television" and we should call it what it really is—a venue where "journalists" not only ask questions, they answer them too.

Jack Shafer did a piece for *Slate* quoting an article by the late novelist David Foster Wallace. "It's obvious that FOX News Channel and its imitators have incorporated many of talk radio's basic lessons into their architecture…These radio and cable entertainers do precisely what they damn mainstream media reporters for doing. They interpret, analyze, and explain news inside their narrow political context." And they do it with perpetual rage that "throbs with the dark fury of an aneurysm in Joe Sixpack's brain… It's unlikely any middle-aged man could go around this upset all the time and not drop dead."[101]

While content was "king" at the FOX News Channel, beauty was "queen." Most of the women behind the anchor desk were variations on a theme. Blond hair and great legs were job prerequisites. Nevertheless, many of their anchorwomen were intelligent and effective. Megyn Kelly and Alisyn Camerota proved beauty and brains are a formidable combination. Camerota moved on to become the respected cohost of *New Day* on CNN. Kelly's departure did not end as well. She went from moderating presidential debates to a softball talk show that NBC unceremoniously canceled. Martha MacCallum and Dana Perino stayed at FOX and remain popular.

As FOX News Channel expanded its reach, the Roger Ailes formula was working despite criticism from liberal and middle-of-the-road purists. Distribution expanded and ratings climbed, as witness the success of Bill O'Reilly. Formerly at ABC News, O'Reilly ditched the role of network correspondent and became an evangelist riling up the congregation to a fever pitch. His show was many things to many people, but it definitely was not a "no-spin zone," even though he told us it was every night. Soon O'Reilly had the highest-rated primetime news program on cable. For FNC, those were the glory days, but later O'Reilly and Ailes both left the network in disgrace after numerous charges of sexual harassment.

If Fox News Channel marked a nuclear explosion in the television news universe, competing cable channels were contaminated by the fallout. CUNY Professor Reece Peck writes, "All this energy spent in unmasking FOX's political agenda, its comic ridiculousness, and its unprofessionalism has done little to diminish its influence or ratings, nor has it yielded a satisfactory answer to the question of why this overtly conservative network was able to move from the periphery of the national public sphere to the center, transforming the entire ecology of the US news environment in the process."[102]

For those who fear for the soul of America, the fault—dear reader—lies not only in cable stars but also in ourselves. Just observe the chanting crowds at Trump rallies. Perhaps FOX astutely sensed latent anger and tapped into it. Perhaps its audience was ready made, waiting to be unleashed.

As FOX continued to dominate the ratings war, its competitors' high-minded resolve to avoid partisanship began to erode. MSNBC was next to venture into the primetime "dark side." Gradually, their front page became their editorial page. They no longer attempted to be a DMZ, an opinion-free zone. Their strategy worked to a limited degree as their numbers improved, but FOX continued to dominate the ratings sweepstakes. "There is simply nothing comparable on the left. No mainstream left-of-center media organization, however broadly you define that category, that departs so willingly and extensively from journalism's fundamental mission to report facts as fairly and objectively as possible." That analysis from *The FOX Effect* authors David Brock and Ari Rabin-Havt.[103]

Writing in the *Columbia Journalism Review*, Jacob Nelson quotes media scholar Laura Feldman. "While MSNBC is certainly partisan and traffics in outrage and opinion, its reporting—even on its primetime talk shows—has a much cleaner relationship with facts than does coverage on FOX." Princeton professor Andy Guess also draws a clear distinction between FOX and its liberal competitors. "There's no doubt that primetime hosts on FOX News are increasingly comfortable trafficking in conspiracy theories and open appeals to nativism, which is a major difference from its liberal counterparts."[104]

Unbiased reporters have three major goals: uncover truth, inform the public, and safeguard democracy. But their bosses, the top-level executives who operate media companies, are focused on something entirely different. They're running a business—eager to make profits and accountable to shareholders. They care more about the bottom line than the byline. And therein lies the rub. Reporters are hunting for facts, while media moguls are hunting for profits. In television news, profits are determined by one thing—Nielsen ratings. As Chris Wallace, the brightest light at FOX, boasted to Jon Stewart on *The Daily Show*, "We had the highest ratings. More ratings than CNN and MSNBC combined." That's a very big deal.

I participated in the ratings game for four decades. We were constantly looking in the rearview mirror, not second-guessing our reports but second-guessing our ratings. In retrospect, it's sad to reflect on the lengths local news executives went to boost the almighty ratings. If network news was deadly serious, local news had a lighter touch. They hired high-priced consultants who suggested a simple four-word formula for achieving Nielsen's Nirvana. "Tits. Tots. Pets. Vets." Translation: do stories about sexy women, cute toddlers, household pets, and heroic veterans. And they were serious.

Why would professional journalists turn to market researchers for editorial guidance? We're supposed to be the pros. But some of the station executives who commissioned those surveys weren't reporters by trade. They were salesmen who rose through the bureaucracy to wield power. I was never privy to the invoice, but I'm willing to bet we paid handsomely for that not-so-sage advice.

Every day around three o'clock, we fixated on last night's "numbers" as the Nielsens were distributed. In the old days, an intern with a stack of xeroxes went from desk to desk handing them out. As computers proliferated, we read our fate online. How did we do last night? Did we kill? Or did we die? These were serious questions and our professional futures could be in jeopardy if the ratings tanked for any length of time, especially during the key ratings periods called "sweeps." Nielsen families, who share their viewing habits with the ratings service, are carefully selected to represent a larger segment of the population. Sometimes when our numbers dipped, we joked, "The 30-something Protestant couple from Bronxville must have gone out to dinner." Attempts at newsroom humor are a release valve for the tragic stories we cover and the unrelenting pressure to be number one.

Frank Sesno, who covered Washington heavyweights for CNN, addressed the linkage between the quest for ratings and the viewers' perceptions of the media. "The 'if it bleeds, it leads' syndrome may boost ratings, but it doesn't help advance the image of responsible journalism or even commitment to community...I refer to distrust of the media as a 'preexisting condition.' The public has long held media in some measure of scorn, feeling they are biased or superficial, negative or narrow. Some of that is justifiable because much of the news is out of step with people's experience."

But now the competition for viewers has a very dangerous dimension, because we have a ratings-obsessed reality television star in the Oval Office. Disgruntled *Apprentice* insiders say there was panic in Trump Tower when their ratings slipped. Margaret Sullivan told me, "Trump has called himself a ratings machine and he is right. There's something about him that's compelling to the television audience...He was great for ratings and ratings matter in TV. You know, that's understandable. But when a person becomes a candidate to become the leader of the free world, it seems different rules should apply."

Figuring out those new rules proved a tricky proposition that became more complex during the coronavirus pandemic. Daily briefings put Donald Trump in the spotlight, and his ratings skyrocketed. Rather than ignore the numbers and focus on the medical crisis, he bragged his ratings were higher than *The Bachelor* and he ranked number one on Facebook. Those self-aggrandizing remarks demonstrated the measure of the man, and Donald Trump did not measure up to presidential standards. Just as narcissism dominated *The Apprentice*, it dominated his approach to a worldwide disaster. The plague was all about him, not about us. Networks found themselves in a Catch-22. If they broadcast the sessions, their numbers soared and so did their ad revenue. True, the public had a right to know, a right to hear their president address the crisis. But did that make newscasts complicit? Donald Trump's accessories after the fact?

Jeff Zucker, the powerful executive who runs CNN, previously headed NBC Entertainment, where he oversaw *The Apprentice* as Donald Trump cemented his superstar status. Ironically, media brass at all three cable news networks burnished Trump's image during the 2016 campaign by giving him an overabundance of airtime. That exposure was priceless and no doubt elevated Trump to the ranks of serious contenders. FOX had ideological motives. CNN and MSNBC did it for ratings, because even people who wouldn't vote for Donald Trump were fascinated enough to watch him on TV as he launched his political career.

Phil Griffin is president of MSNBC. He guided the network from its infancy to an elevated profile by experimenting with different formulas to boost ratings. He once told Bill Carter of *The New York Times*, "We've got to adjust. We've got to evolve." That meant shuffling the lineup more than once, searching for the right combination. Not only did new hosts appear, new formats did too. *The Rachel Maddow Show* is calculated in style and substance to present an anti-FOX, anti-Trump alternative and attract the prized 25–54 demographic. Advertisers are eager to reach those eyeballs and willing to pay higher commercial rates.

Some MSNBC anchors have resisted the "tit for tat" war of words. Andrea Mitchell runs a very tight ship patterned on the unbiased newscasts we used to expect. She personifies everything that journalism should be. Brian Williams's nightly program *The Eleventh Hour* is the closest thing to a traditional newscast on late-night cable. He projects gravitas and his guests demonstrate more substance than flash. Nicolle Wallace, who was the White House Communications Director for George W. Bush and a senior advisor on the John McCain presidential campaign, calls 'em like she sees 'em on her MSNBC program even when it conflicts with the GOP party line she once supported. "I come at everything from the perspective of having been covered…I know the difference between a favorable spin or a favorable presentation of facts and a lie…When the spin crosses the border into a lie, I want to stand up and scream liar, liar, pants on fire."[105]

Even die-hard liberals don't defend MSNBC's *Morning Joe* as "unbiased," but it is a provocative way to start the day. Loyal viewers, this author included, open one eye and reach for the remote. Several years ago, cohosts Joe Scarborough and Mika Brzezinski were buddies of Donald Trump. Later, they traded nasty personal insults. But their team is balanced by solid, impartial Willie Geist and sagacious Mike Barnicle, plus semiregular panelists of stature including Peter Baker, Michael Beschloss, David Ignatius, Walter Isaacson, John Heilemann, John Meacham, Peggy Noonan, and Eugene Robinson.

Change.org, which is a generally acknowledged liberal website, blasted Scarborough and Brzezinski, charging that their attacks on Donald Trump "taint the process of journalism and ethics. We need to hold them accountable. They need to be fired."[106] The anchor duo defended their actions in an interview with the *Harvard Political Review*. Brzezinski said, "It's really hard to limit bias, but what you can do is control it, [maintain] a sense of objectivity and open-ness towards different points of view…Joe's a Republican turned Independent and I'm a Democrat and everybody knows that." Scarborough said, "None of us are sitting there trying to be the voice of God and pretending that we're objective because nobody is."[107] Unlike *FOX & Friends*, it's important to note *Morning Joe* may be heavy on opinion, but it's also heavy on facts.

In the drift toward opinionated coverage, CNN held out the longest, walking that fine line between front-page reporting and editorial-page advocacy. Eventually they metaphorically screamed "Basta!" perhaps driven over the edge by President Trump's vicious taunts of "fake news." In addition, they were getting pummeled in the ratings, so they too veered left. At first, the powers that be ex-ecuted the move with finesse. Most of the blatant criticism came from panelists who were clearly identified as partisans.

CNN anchors Kate Bolduan, Erin Burnett, Anderson Cooper, Chris Cuomo, Don Lemon, and Jake Tapper pride themselves on ask-ing tough questions. Supporters praise them, but some critics equate CNN's tenacity with political bias. Veteran anchor Wolf Blitzer, rock-solid Jim Scuitto, and John Berman play it straight without in-jecting persistent commentary. Rounding out the reporting team, Christiane Amanpour, Dana Bash, Gloria Borger, Pamela Browne, Shimon Prokupecz, Manu Raju, and Barbara Starr are "old school," and that's a compliment. Simultaneously, CNN recruited many of the best analysts in the business, including Carl Bernstein, Maggie Haberman, Juliette Kayyem, Philip Mudd, Ana Navarro, Jeffrey Toobin, and the four Davids—Gergen, Axelrod, Gregory, and Chalian.

CNN has been targeted by President Trump as a repository of "fake news." Anchor Anderson Cooper is the recipient of many accolades, including the Walter Cronkite Award for Excellence in

Journalism. In his acceptance speech, he told the audience, "There is truth and there are lies. There is fact and there is fiction and it's our job to point that out even if it seems at times no one is listening."

However, the need for objectivity may no longer be an absolute. It's being debated and reassessed even by purists. Larry Sabato told me, "The problem with CNN, with the exception of a few people, is that their MO is to pretend they can present both sides and that both sides are worthy. No, both sides are not worthy, and I am shocked that I'm saying this because I preached for years that you have to be balanced to the degree that you can be. But this president presents a dilemma for everybody, not just the news media but the pundits and citizens and just about everybody. Because telling the truth means being unbalanced, period…This man [Donald Trump] is a threat to our institutions and our fundamentals and if you don't rein him in, there is a real chance he will not vacate the office on time and be supported, as a University of Virginia poll showed. About a third of his own party support not leaving the White House on time."

In the autumn of 2018, in the run-up to the midterm elections, there was an interesting twist in cable news coverage. The dynamic of the Trump–FOX alliance frayed slightly as the conservative network cut back live coverage of Trump's campaign rallies because viewership was declining. The move was proof-positive that ratings are the ultimate criteria. Rival networks CNN and MSNBC seized the opportunity to cut back their rally coverage. But their motives may have been equal parts ideology and ratings-driven.

Sometimes journalists can boost their ratings simply by letting viewers set the agenda. Give them what they want and feed the hungry beast. FOX viewers hungered for dirt on Barack Obama, and the network obliged by hyping the birther controversy and trying to turn the Solera investigation into a major scandal. Later, during the 2016 presidential race, FOX hammered away at Hillary Clinton, reporting ad nauseam on Benghazi and the FBI investigation of her emails. Those issues warranted legitimate coverage, but this was overkill as FNC stoked the partisan fire knowing it would incense GOP voters and pay off with higher ratings. Later, MSNBC and CNN followed suit by hyping the Mueller probe into possible Russian collusion with the Trump campaign. All three news outlets discovered that dual objectives sometimes coalesce. It's possible to stake out a position and boost your ratings simultaneously.

Something else to consider is the role FOX plays in setting policy for the Trump administration. In the past, presidents befriended some reporters, but the ground rules were different. President John F. Kennedy and Ben Bradlee were close friends, and that worked to Bradlee's advantage. He had the inside track on access and exclusives, but Bradlee never dictated policy. Today, Donald Trump's alliance with FOX crosses a line, and sometimes it's hard to tell if Sean Hannity and *FOX & Friends* are reporting policies or instigating them.

That raises serious questions. Who's calling the shots? Who's crafting the agenda? There were numerous occasions when FOX personalities spoke directly to their "audience of one" in the Oval Office and later in the day President Trump regurgitated their policy suggestions. CNN's Brian Stelter commented on the Trump–FOX connection. "The big questions for newsrooms are: Where did this come from? Who's telling Trump this stuff?…Well, the answer, as is so often the case, is right on FOX News…That's where the president is getting his information…And then Trump tweets an hour later…Donald Trump is getting this distorted view of the country from a right-wing channel."[108]

No wonder Americans on both sides of the political divide have a failure to communicate in an age when some broadcasters don't just report on legislation, they propose it then cheerlead for its implementation. Or, conversely, when they oppose a policy and try to beat it to death. During the healthcare debate, amid fears of "socialized medicine," FOX Vice President Bill Sammons sent emails instructing staffers to parrot GOP language and refer to "the public option" as "the government option." That phrase sounded more ominous and would help get out the vote. It was supremely ironic because many FOX viewers are older and on Medicare, a successful and popular American take on "socialized medicine."

The loyalty of the FOX audience is not unique. MSNBC and CNN have devoted followers who watch because their beliefs skew liberal. Talk to your family and friends and a very clear pattern emerges. People change channels until they find one that reflects their political beliefs. Dr. Larry Sabato believes even when television journalists play it down the middle, "They're not necessarily partisan, but the people watching them are, and they appeal to that audience. They have to if they're going to survive. This is a vicious media world." And the root cause of that viciousness is twofold—partisanship and Nielsen ratings. It's a corrosive combination that distorts unvarnished truth.

Throughout his career, Ted Koppel refused to pander. But he's a realist and knows he was able to stay pure because "*Nightline* made money, therefore we had a certain level of influence and clout...If the *New York Times*'s circulation suddenly started going down and that of the *Washington Post* suddenly started going down and the editors and the publishers and the executives at networks came to the conclusion that the American public was tired of hearing all this stuff and they want something else, do you think they would still be driven by their sense of commitment, by the crusade, or do you think they might start putting some other material in? I have some skepticism that they would continue with a story that people no longer want to hear."[109]

The power of news consumers has increased in tandem with expanded viewing options that were not available during television's infancy and adolescence. The wide range of choices on broadcast, cable, the internet, social media, and print border on intellectual overload, too much information. Television is, perhaps, the most powerful platform of all because the printed word tends to be cerebral while television is visceral. When the Trump administration separated migrant children from their parents, reading about it in the newspaper was disturbing, but not as gut-wrenching as watching the children's tears and hearing their cries on television. This was a legitimate use of emotion to tell the real story. But in the race to win the ratings crown, do journalists routinely exploit ordinary people caught in extraordinary situations? This is an argument the press can't win. Too much coverage is called exploitation, while too little coverage is called incomplete. "The media have come in for a raft of criticism over how they're doing their jobs—no matter how they do it…Critics have pounced on coverage as intrusive, voyeuristic, and ratings-driven."[110]

The landscape is constantly changing as journalists try to function in a world where President Trump runs the country like a bizarre reality show. Some marquee names who initially held the line and reported just the facts are reluctantly voicing opinions after vicious attacks and outrageous lies from an openly hostile administration. The daily routine in television newsrooms has become a delicate balancing act as reporters and producers who simply want to report the news spend endless hours dodging bullets in a perpetual combat zone.

CHAPTER FOUR

OLD SCHOOL, NEW SCHOOL

If cable news is the energetic progeny, broadcast news is its staid grandfather. Long ago in a galaxy far, far away, network news had a monopoly. Viewing options were limited to ABC, CBS, or NBC. The big three networks ran the only games in town and their news operations ruled the airwaves. Nightly news was a valued and valuable commodity. It was considered the network's crown jewel—establishing identity, boosting credibility, and making money. That was a television trifecta and those were the glory days. CBS correspondent Marvin Kalb recalls a meeting where CBS owner and Chairman William Paley told reporters not to be concerned about costs, saying, "I have Jack Benny to make money."[111] That philosophy is a reminder of how drastically the dynamics have changed.

Nightly newscasts aired around dinnertime, and for many Americans it was appointment viewing. Anchoring the news was considered the ultimate golden ring. Anchormen were stars, household names pontificating from ivory towers with authority and neutrality. In the 1960s and 1970s, the revered oracles were Walter Cronkite at CBS, Howard K. Smith at ABC, and Chet Huntley and David Brinkley at NBC. In a later era, Dan Rather took the helm at CBS, Peter Jennings was behind the desk at ABC, and Tom Brokaw became the voice of NBC. Network anchors possessed gravitas and integrity. Those qualities were job prerequisites, along with experience and an adequate amount of hair. Before they took the helm, anchormen were well-seasoned reporters who dodged bullets in combat zones and maneuvered through Washington's corridors of power.

Those generations of network news anchors were "absolute kings of the American media universe, with audiences that today are almost unimaginable. It was the most prestigious job in American journalism, in part because there were only three of them."[112] They were all male, all white, roughly the same age, surrounded by producers who mirrored the same demographic profile.

Consuelo Mack is anchor of the weekly PBS program *Wealthtrack with Consuelo Mack*. She previously anchored *The Wall Street Journal Report*. "The old system [consisted] of a very small group of white men, many from the same backgrounds, deciding what we heard and saw. However, TV news divisions were seen as a necessary and essential service for democracy, not just for revenue, entertainment and ratings. Now the mission and greater sense of purpose have been overshadowed by ratings and entertainment...What's happening is not all negative, because now we have multiple choices on TV and radio and on the internet. There is so much more information enabling us to be better informed if citizens make the effort. Few do, few ever have."

When network news ruled the airwaves, it was almost impossible for women to break through the glass ceiling. At first, networks took the safe approach, dipping their toes in the pool by pairing prominent women journalists with a solid male coanchor.

Barbara Walters led the way in 1976 when ABC News paired her with Harry Reasoner, who was less than welcoming. It was an important first step but implied a woman couldn't or shouldn't go it alone. Later, networks took the plunge and cast women solo, including Connie Chung, Katie Couric, Diane Sawyer, and Jessica Savitch.

Anchoring the news depends on the cult of personality to attract and retain a core audience. Who do you trust in times of crisis when citizens need information and reassurance? Sitting behind the anchor desk is a high-stakes game of musical chairs. At the moment of this writing, Norah O'Donnell is center stage at CBS, Lester Holt at NBC, David Muir at ABC, and Judy Woodruff on PBS.

David Muir at *ABC World News Tonight* admits he has big shoes to fill. "I think about it every day, to be honest with you. I'm fully aware that when I go upstairs—that same stairwell that Peter Jennings took and Charlie Gibson took and Diane Sawyer took—up to that desk, that I'm having a conversation with America at a very polarized time...We're all aware of ratings. And all I can say is that I'm grateful that people seem to be responding. The thing that does it for me is to reinforce the responsibility we have every night to break through the noise. They're bombarded all day long with tweets or abbreviated forms of news and [we] try to help them decipher what matters."[113]

Lester Holt deciphers events at rival *NBC Nightly News*. "I do think it's healthy that people become critical thinkers and question what they read and some of what they see. But from our perspective, we combat that by being more transparent, talking more about how we source our stories. We don't rely generally on a single source. Telling people as much as we can about the process of where this information comes from—I think that is something we do on a normal basis, but in this time of heightened skepticism, we can't do it enough…Mine is a straightforward hard newscast. While we provide analysis, we don't provide opinion."[114]

Norah O'Donnell is the newest anchor in town at *CBS Evening News*. In a revolutionary twist, she was hired by the first woman president of CBS News, Susan Zirinsky. Both women follow in the footsteps of a male-dominated tradition. O'Donnell closed her debut newscast by quoting broadcast trailblazer Edward R. Murrow on the power of television. "This instrument can teach, it can illuminate, and it can inspire. But it can only do it to the extent that humans are determined to use it to those ends. Otherwise, it is nothing but wires and lights in a box. There is a great and perhaps decisive battle to be fought against ignorance, intolerance, and indifference. This weapon of television could be useful." [115]

Today's network anchors are excellent and respected journalists who worked hard to earn their coveted spots. But times and viewing patterns have changed and competition is everywhere. Today, the average American may not recognize their names or their faces. The age of Walter Cronkite is history. And while network news is still credible, touches of commercialism are evident, fueled by the circus-like antics of Donald Trump.

Ted Koppel is quite harsh in his assessment of network news. "One day, we're going to be in a post-Trump era and we will be left with the residue from what we have created and what we are creating today. And, you know, watch NBC News, watch CBS News, watch ABC News. I mean broadcast news. Talk about drivel…They're trying very hard not to do critical pieces on Donald Trump every night. The end result is they're doing weather shows, fire shows, winsome little children who have some physical hand-icap...And I find myself sitting there, my wife and I sit there and say, 'How the hell is that the most important thing going on in the world today?'"[116] His former colleague Jeff Greenfield agrees. "This, to me, is a really critical point and it is a shock. I know this begins to sound like, you know, the ocean was better in the old days. But...my wife and I, sometimes we watch network news, and basically, after ten minutes, it's car crashes, it's dramatic se-curity camera footage of somebody hitting somebody else. And our former ABC and CNN guy, Aaron Brown, who grew up in Minnesota, used to say he wanted to go on the air one night and say, 'It's January. It snows in January. It snows a lot. Here's the [real] news.'"[117]

Don't get me started on weather. At *Eyewitness News* we'd lead the newscast with live shots from snow-related traffic jams in the New York–New Jersey area. I always wondered, *who really cares?* If you're watching at home nestled before a fire, so what if there's a traffic jam thirty miles away? And if you're stuck in traffic, the report is meaningless because you couldn't access television from your stalled car in those days. But top brass looked at the Nielsen ratings and determined viewers liked weather stories, so we gave the public what it wanted.

For decades, network rivals ABC, CBS, and NBC have been locked in nightly battles for the hearts and minds of America—and the coveted Nielsen crown. Although premier anchors refrained from voicing opinions, media critics and the public suspected, often with good reason, that the press tilted left. If you paid very close attention, there were subliminal messages, but there was no openly "liberal" network, no openly "conservative" network.

According the Pew Research Center, "Network journalism, built around visual storytelling, still tends to take viewers to the events of the world outside. Cable news, built around talk-show hosts, tends to take viewers into the studio. In this new TV journalism there is a sense the news is secondary to the staged debate about the news. Network journalism originally was designed not to make a profit but to create prestige. Cable is all about profit and keeping costs low. What is disappearing is an idealism about the potential of TV as a medium to better our politics and society."[118]

A Rand Corporation Report that relied heavily on statistical research concluded, "Journalism in the US has become more subjective and consists less of the detailed event or context-based reporting that used to characterize news coverage…Before 2000, broadcast news segments were more likely to include relatively complex academic and precise language, as well as complex reasoning. After 2000, broadcast news becomes less preplanned as on-air personalities engaged in conversations."[119] The year 2000 is a significant line of demarcation. Viewership of television news increased as the Bush v. Gore election made headlines. It dragged on for weeks and was ultimately decided by the Supreme Court, a watershed moment that directly affected the news we see twenty years later on broadcast and cable outlets.

The Rand report also concludes, "Comparing broadcast news to cable programming, the differences become more stark, with cable segments dedicating more time to opinion coverage and using argumentative language. The size and scope of these changes is substantial, but researchers also noted that these differences may be in part a result of their different audiences, with cable focusing on specialized [partisan] audiences."[120]

Katy Tur views it this way: "Cable is different from network news. Both breed intimacy because both come right into your home, often during dinner or breakfast or some other moment when domestic life is happening, and attendance is invite only. But network morning and evening shows are only on during particular windows and there's a lot less audience loyalty than you might imagine. Every day, or almost every day, you're addressing millions of people you're meeting for what might be the first time. That's not true on cable. Cable is on all day. Viewers know you like they know their own family. When you're doing live shots every hour, your personality bleeds through. There is nowhere to hide and, even if there were, you'd be too tired to hide there."[121]

"Take a look at cable," Ted Koppel says. "Take a look at how many men and women are on cable television trying to whip up your anger, trying to get you really furious. Why? Because it sells and it's cheap. It's a lot cheaper to put five people around a table yelling at each other than it is to have [foreign correspondents]. When I was a young foreign correspondent, ABC, NBC, and CBS among the three of them probably had in excess of one hundred foreign correspondents based all over the world telling you on a nightly basis what was happening in those different regions that might ultimately be of importance to us as a nation. You know what ABC and NBC and CBS now have? Probably, collectively among the three of them, fewer than twenty. Why? Because it's expensive to have foreign correspondents overseas. But put half a dozen people around a table yelling at each other. That's cheap. Costs nothing. Nothing. And, apparently, it's entertaining."[122]

"The networks argue that they don't need as many bureaus and reporters because their role has changed. Rather than trying to be the first on the air with a headline or picture, the mission at ABC,

CBS, and NBC is defined as providing extra-value-added programming, in-depth analysis, and original reporting that twenty-four-hour cable services and local TV can't duplicate. This makes sense, but it's difficult to provide thoughtful reporting of stories around the nation and the world without reporters on the ground who are given resources to develop expertise."[123]

Paul Friedman, who once served as executive producer of *ABC World News Tonight*, thinks, "If you have good people who have a lot of experience, you can generally parachute in and do a good job. But it is not the same as having somebody on the ground who calls you and says, you know, you really ought to...take a look at this developing story. The same goes for Washington, where specialized beats have been gradually eliminated or several assignments have been combined."[124]

In its heyday, watching network news bordered on a religious ritual for families from coast to coast. But now audiences are steadily declining as younger Americans get their news from digital platforms. Because demographics are changing and older viewers are literally dying off, traditional newscasts may be teetering on the verge of extinction. How long will cost-conscious networks fund their news divisions when cable news is where the action is? Ted Koppel knows well the importance of profitability and thinks network brass "are terrified that they're going to lose the last couple of million people that they have left."[125]

However, network news programs got a significant boost during the coronavirus pandemic. Historically, in times of crisis, American voters tend to watch more TV news and tend to stand by their president, fueled by a desire to overcome a common enemy that threatens our nation. Perhaps that contributed to a temporary bounce in Donald Trump's poll numbers. Many politicians and journalists were critical of his policies and performance, but initially Trump's favorability numbers went up. And so did the ratings. What was good for Donald Trump was proving good for network news as the number of viewers climbed to levels television executives only dream about. The resurgence of network news at a perilous time may reflect the public's desire for solid unvarnished information minus the acrimonious cable confrontations that can raise anxiety levels rather than calm them.

Many factors contribute to the viability and profitability of broadcast news. Over the years, ownership of the major networks changed hands and the first order of business for most new management teams was formulaic—cut the budget. When I worked at *Eyewitness News* at WABC in New York City in the 1980s, those were the gravy days when money was flowing. When I arrived, a top news exec sat me down and told me, "We get the news first and we get it best. And money is no problem." I could charter a helicopter unilaterally and there was minimal red tape to charter fixed-wing planes. During my tenure, the company was sold to cost-conscious Capital Cities. By the time I left, things had changed. I was producing a Sunday-morning political program, *Eyewitness News Conference*. It was a local version of *Meet the Press*. Mayor Ed Koch was a regular guest, and a greenroom ritual had evolved. We provided tea and cookies and chatted about movies. After the taping, I submitted a seven-dollar deli receipt and was called on the carpet and told to "cut expenses." Choppers were definitely out and apparently so were tea and cookies. That story is a tiny vignette, but it crystalizes the dimensions of serious budget slashing that plagued all three networks. In the 1980s and 1990s, international and domestic bureaus were closed or consolidated. Staff layoffs and hiring freezes were routine. Unions were strong-armed. Programs were canceled. It was an era when times were tough behind the scenes.

The network news you see on your television screen is determined by anchors and reporters you know and producers and executives you don't know. There are hundreds of broadcast journalists who make editorial judgments all day every day. Like so many other professions, journalists make choices. Lawyers choose to accept or decline cases and carefully select juries and witnesses. Doctors weigh options before they prescribe medication, surgery, or physical therapy. These choices are rooted in professional expertise. While they are subjective, they're not inherently biased. The same is true of broadcast journalism, where our choices sometimes begin weeks in advance. We keep "futures" files on newsroom computers alerting us to upcoming events. Planning ahead whenever possible can generate in-depth reports and award-winning exposés. Did you ever wonder why an obit is almost instantaneous when a famous person dies? Some obituary tributes are pre-edited and waiting to air.

In addition to long-range planning, there's a standard day-of-air routine. The tempo is similar to a symphony that starts adagio, then builds to a frenetic crescendo. The day begins with the hallowed morning meeting. Participants come prepared with facts and ideas. It's the place choices are made about what to cover and how to cover it.

Katie Tur wrote about it in her book *Unbelievable*, "The Exchange is NBC's name for our morning editorial meeting. All the executives, show heads, senior producers, bureau chiefs, and correspondents hoping to get on television that day must either be in that room or dialed in by phone."[126]

Potential stories are pitched and the ensuing debate can be thoughtful and congenial. But sometimes the dialogue gets heated as staffers jockey to be the smartest voice in the room and maneuver for the next big promotion. Below the surface, there are long-standing alliances and deep-seated rivalries. To lighten the mood, there are moments of comic relief. There's no hard-and-fast quota, but every newsroom has at least one resident comedian who cleverly channels Colbert or *Saturday Night Live* at just the right moment to break the tension.

The goal of the morning meeting is to create a road map by agreeing what to cover and how to cover it. Will a reporter be assigned to dig out exclusive facts on location? If so, which reporter? Generally it's the "beat" reporter who knows the terrain and has relationships with key players. Or will we downplay less-important events by simply sending a camera crew to get generic video and record public statements at a staged news conference? As the day progresses, more choices are made, primarily by the producer of the newscast, who crafts the "rundown." The rundown lists each report in order of importance and calculates the precise timing of each segment. Additional decisions are made throughout the day as producers select which stories to add or cut and what to promote heavily to attract viewers at night.

In addition to editorial content, cosmetic choices are made. What does the set look like? Is it edgy or is it staid? As graphics appear on-screen, what colors have been selected and what subliminal messages do they send? Urgency or reassurance? The same applies to theme music. These choices sometimes rely on market research, but ultimately the final decisions are subjective. By the time viewers see the animated show open and hear the familiar theme music, literally dozens of choices have been made—decisions based on experience and editorial judgment, not partisan politics.

The esteemed BBC published its editorial guidelines. "When [we] report a story, the aim is to provide insight based on evidence

and on professional judgment—uncluttered by commercial interest or the need to support a particular proprietor or ideology. We
should not be driven by what other media organizations are saying
about a story. Nor should we assess a story's importance by mea-
suring the prominence it is given elsewhere. We need to work out
for ourselves what matters and what is just spin, public relations or
chaff...We should not be frightened by controversy, but we should
always be alert to the dangers of glibness, to the idea that every
problem has a simple solution. So above all, we need to be inquiring
and open-minded, unafraid to surprise our audiences with a view
of a story that is different—and always looking for a wide range of
evidence and opinion."[127]

After producers meticulously sort through evidence and opinion, breaking news can erupt during a live newscast. Preplanning
goes out the window and spur-of-the-moment decisions are made
in real time in the control room and at the anchor desk. Sometimes,
the original rundown melts down completely as breaking events
consume large portions of the program. Talk about tension. That
part of the job is simultaneously exhausting and exhilarating—and
requires nerves of steel.

"When broadcast journalists get to work on breaking news, it's a
moment that always separates mere readers from true leaders. The
best news anchors and live reporters make their work look easy, but
it isn't. Beyond voice, looks, delivery, the best possess...'skills without scripts.' When all hell is breaking loose, journalists are the calm
in the eye of the storm."[128]

But if news doesn't break during the program, we stick to Plan
A and meticulously crafted scripts magically pop up on the teleprompter. Network news programs run a scant thirty minutes
and are tightly scripted down to the second. The production staff

has all day to get it together, in sharp contrast to cable's rapid-fire turnarounds. The biggest upside to a slower pace is accuracy, since there's plenty of time to check and double-check facts, to edit and reedit tape, to write and rewrite copy. Wording is important. An event can be labeled "troubling" or "suspicious" or "inflammatory," all implying different shades of interpretation. The late Rebecca Lipkin, a dear friend who worked at *Eyewitness News* then transitioned to *ABC World News Tonight*, told me she wrote a script for Peter Jennings then had a conference call with Jennings and his executive producer. They carefully debated the pros and cons of one word. Should the script read that something "might" happen or that it "could" happen? Talk about precision. In the current whirlwind of perpetually "breaking" news that's a lost luxury and a lost art.

Journalists who make the transition from local or cable news to network news instinctively feel the differences. And so do viewers. Local news tends to be folksy and friendly with news-you-can-use and softball features. Network news tends to be serious, focusing on big-picture national and global events.

Neal Shapiro is the current president of the PBS affiliate in New York and the former head of NBC News. At a Pew Research Center summit a number of years ago, he said, "I think network news still has to appeal to the widest possible audience, and the way to do that is to try to be as conclusive as possible and report without bias and to work damn hard to keep whatever biases exist out of the story. I don't think that will change at a network."[129]

As Consuelo Mack points out, "Edward R. Murrow took sides in World War II but was not fired because he was popular and drew large audiences. And turns out he was right." Looking ahead to how network news might evolve, Mack believes, "*The Wall Street Journal* is a model for the future—unbiased reporting in the paper with a clearly defined and separate editorial section." That would bring broadcasts full circle back to the days of Cronkite with the news and Sevareid with the commentary. It was a formula that worked then and might work now.

When Seymour Hersh surveys news operations around the world, he concludes, "I do not pretend to have an answer to the problems of the media today. Should the government underwrite the media as England does with the BBC? Ask Donald Trump about that."[130]

Love him or hate him, President Trump has become the centerpiece of network news by virtue of his office and erratic persona. However, even Donald Trump, a human ratings machine, may not be enough to rescue network news from declining viewership and declining revenue. The demographics are a powerful force as millennials veto broadcast news as too old school, then click on omnipresent mobile devices searching for new-school sources. First network news had to contend with competition from cable; now it's under attack from the internet and hipper outlets on demand.

Jeff Gralnick is a news executive who has worked at high levels at all three networks. "If they adapt, [network] brands might survive. The merging of forms being made both possible and necessary by digital and wireless reach mandates that all of the traditional and mainstream [outlets] find ways to distribute themselves in nontraditional ways or they will die. The smart networks will, and will see the need to invest ahead of provable or visible Return on Investment. The rest will die."[131]

Speaking at a Pew forum, Neal Shapiro agreed. "In the long run, they will have to do that…New media and old media will exist together for a while, and the branding of the old media may make the difference about who survives and who doesn't."[132]

Tom Bettag, who was executive producer of *Nightline*, also participated in the Pew symposium. He thinks, "Many organizations will not pass the test. Those that do will become invaluable at times of national emergency when it's critical to be able to get accurate information. Ultimately, the networks will do whatever it takes to make money. Advertisers are moving to the web. There is money to be made, and these organizations do not lack for business savvy."[133]

Cognizant of the generational shift to digital sources, Ted Koppel urges network news divisions to "Offer something a little more interesting, a little more substantive, and something that answers the question: 'What do I have after half an hour of watching your program that I didn't know beforehand?'" Jeff Greenfield is on the same page. "I actually took the step of writing a colleague who has now taken over a major news network and said, 'Why don't you try an evening news with maybe three stories? Maybe like the old *Nightline*-length stories? Maybe follow it with a little context and just scrap the old [format]?'...It strikes me, measured by their own metrics, that if you could do an evening news show that said to people 'we're going to try to actually do this in a way that you might find worthy of attention,' they could make a lot of money."[134]

While revenue from staid network newscasts is flat or declining, somebody out there is making money. Enter late-night night satire à la Stephen Colbert and Trevor Noah, direct descendants of David Letterman and Jon Stewart. If broadcast news makes us cry, late-night comedy makes us laugh at the absurdity of our politics and our politicians. And not just Donald Trump. There's plenty of material out there in local, state, and federal governments. For political junkies who appreciate acerbic wit, late-night TV is a bedtime ritual, especially for younger viewers who trust Colbert more than all the network anchors combined.

While some viewers are addicted to late night, early risers start the day with their morning show of choice. The NBC website refers to *Today* as a news program that sets the agenda for the rest of the day. When they land a newsmaker exclusive, it qualifies as news. But live concerts and endless segments on fashion, travel and celebrities—not so much. Same thing at ABC, where *Good Morning America* bounced from the entertainment division to the news division, perpetuating the glitz by airing too many soft features and not enough hard news. *CBS This Morning* seems newsier, with some standout correspondents, including legal analyst Rikki Klieman.

For hardcore politicos, MSNBC and CNN offer excellent morning options. On CNN's *New Day*, John Berman and Alisyn Camerota are sober and reflective, as are Mike Barnicle and Willie Geist on MSNBC's *Morning Joe*. But cohosts Joe and Mika throw punches. I say that even though I agree with many of their opinions. In contrast, at the FOX News Channel, the popular *FOX & Friends* is a wake-up call for conservatives who want their morning coffee with heavy doses of partisan jargon.

Over the weekend, the big three networks air Sunday-morning political programs that are cheap to produce and often break news. For years, they were must-see TV for influential newsmakers and informed voters. *Meet the Press, This Week with George Stephanopoulos,* CBS's *Face the Nation* and *FOX News Sunday* are likely to survive in their less competitive and less lucrative weekend time slots. Networks traditionally count on weekend public interest programming to enhance credibility and identity. CBS, the Tiffany network, gets that in spades from the venerable and award-winning *Sunday Morning* and *60 Minutes*, which bookend their Sunday daytime block.

Network primetime magazine programs have relatively modest budgets compared to dramas, comedies, and reality TV. So a few old favorites continue to survive, especially the gold standard *60 Minutes* that just keeps on ticking. *Frontline* on PBS is an hour-long investigative documentary and excellent example of what network journalism can and should be. *Dateline* on NBC and *48 Hours* on CBS have aired important investigations over the years. But now both programs rely heavily on true crime that borders on Lifetime's damsel-in-distress formula. At ABC, *20/20* has shelves full of Emmys. They cover crime in a more compelling and constructive manner by exploring broader criminal justice issues, thanks in large part to ABC senior producer Teri Whitcraft.

One cost-saving benefit of magazine programs is they amass libraries of evergreen features that can be repeated or repackaged, saving time and money. Network magazines, evening newscasts, and morning shows are all tried-and-true formats. But in our brave new world, are they reliable options that will survive, or dinosaurs verging on extinction? And if they do disappear, what replaces them?

Veteran executive Jeff Gralnick, whose career spanned more than half a century at all three major networks, remains convinced that "The economics of declining broadcast audiences and the power of local stations and station groups are going to mandate, at some point, that news at dinner hour disappear and be replaced by some other forms the networks will have to invent." Neal Shapiro voiced similar concerns. "I think the future is online and the phone, the PDA, or any remote device."[135]

Andrew Tyndall, who monitors all three nightly newscasts in his *Tyndall Report*, believes, "As for the…quest for a [younger] audience, I can only reiterate what the evening newscasts do wrong—air at 6:30 p.m., too early, and sell advertising to pharmaceutical firms featuring sick, wrinkly people whose bodies are falling apart." He also thinks story selection must skew younger: "…Too much health and medicine. That point is only a nuance and is hardly a factor. But the first and second problems can be solved by the online innovations—time sharing, ad stripping, unbundling."[136]

Another thing to consider is star power—the cult of personality that compels us to stop what we're doing and grab the remote. Today's network anchors are experienced, diligent, and likable, but don't rank with media giants of the past or have the recognition factor of their contemporary cable counterparts. Those yardsticks may seem superficial, but they're realistic. Even Ted Koppel admits, "I fully understand that we are and always have been and always will be...one part show business."[137] Neither Koppel nor this writer are advocating for Howard Beale clones. But if there is a network news "savior" waiting in the wings, hopefully she or he will prove to be a twenty-first-century version of Murrow, Cronkite, or Koppel.

CHAPTER FIVE

CAN WE PUT THE GENIE BACK IN THE BOTTLE?

For broadcast journalists, these may be the best of times and the worst of times. The best of times because there's no shortage of headlines as events unfold at warp speed. The worst of times because journalists are under attack from accusations of fake news and threats of physical violence. Inevitably, the Trump administration will end, but it will not go gentle into that good night and it threatens to leave a legacy of hate and divisiveness. Donald Trump labeled the press "the enemy of the people." When his administration fades into history, will journalists be viewed as villains or heroes? Will vitriolic exchanges be replaced by civility as cooler tempers and new personalities dominate our national consciousness? That's the best-case scenario. The worst-case scenario is permanent and irrevocable damage to the First Amendment. The late Senator John McCain perceived the danger. He told Chuck Todd on *Meet the*

Press, "The first thing dictators do is shut down the press...We need to learn the lessons of history."[138]

CNN's Jim Acosta has a more positive outlook and predicts the tenor will improve. "As new presidents come along and return a state of normalcy to dealings with the news media, will there be as great a need to stand up for ourselves? Of course not. Playbooks for individual journalists and news organizations will be adjusted accordingly, as we will no longer be under attack...In the decades to come, what in the world will we put in our history books to explain what happened to America? The answer: that depends on what we do right now. Because it's all riding on us...At the end of the day, reporters simply want to write or broadcast a story that tells the American people what's going on in the White House, the United States, and the wider world. That's pretty much it."[139]

But will it be that simple? Is it possible Donald Trump won't really go away? Ted Koppel, not usually an alarmist, warns that the end of the Trump administration may not herald the end of Donald Trump's powerful influence. "Mr. Trump is a brilliant user of social media. I do not believe he would go away in the event he is defeated. Quite the contrary. I think he would form an opposition in exile and would do it far more successfully than the left has done to date."[140]

Might Trump purchase or launch a cable network dedicated to bashing his enemies and emboldening far-right candidates? Might he become FOX News on steroids? Rather than an aberration, we might be witnessing the new normal, with journalists unable to put the genie back in the bottle. It's imperative that the press seize the opportunity to reverse the damage to their credibility, put rancor aside, reject partisanship, and elevate the national dialogue. Ultimately, the future of journalism rests with the working press, from seasoned political reporters to neophytes digging for their first exclusive.

The coming years could be a turning point for journalism, a time when old battles are replaced by new ventures. "Perhaps the traditional American form of journalism has simply been around too long. It seems at times to have grown not just sclerotic but lackluster...Many journalists today remain unable to extricate themselves from the ruins of an old outdated journalism." Strong words from NYU journalism professor Mitchell Stephens, who wrote *Beyond News: The Future of Journalism*. He believes reporters must dig deeper than "who, what, when, and where." They have to emphasize "why" by producing more interpretative stories that require journalists to think more about their reporting, about their use of sources, about their writing...to move beyond a simple stenographic report...not just to distinguish itself on the web but to get smarter, more interesting, better." He advocates "wisdom journalism" a form of reporting that incorporates analysis, meaning, context, and argument combined with explanation and large doses of smart ideas and insight, all presented with honesty, openness, and flexibility." However, Mitchell draws a very clear distinction between "wisdom journalism" and outright bias, never equating the two. He views "wisdom journalism as finding larger issues if not moral themes in contemporary events."[141]

CNN's Brian Stelter thinks journalists should dig deeper than provocative headlines to stress context and patterns. "Is the press up to the challenge?...The pattern is the big story and the challenge for the press is to show the pattern...If we stay focused on the story of the day or the story of week [that's not enough]...Journalists have to keep tracking the pattern that goes back years or decades."[142]

Experts may not agree on solutions, but they generally agree on the problems. Journalism has taken a big hit in recent years. *Business Insider* reported the results of a poll conducted by the Knight Foundation and Gallup. Sixty-two percent of those surveyed believe that television, radio, and newspapers are biased and/or inaccurate. The public's views on impartiality and accuracy often reflect their political beliefs and accordingly their channel of choice. Overall the survey determined that PBS and the Associated Press are considered the least biased outlets by citizens drowning in a sea of information and misinformation.

CNN's Jeffrey Toobin is a champion of a free press, but cautions, "By making occasional mistakes or expressing bias, how badly does the press damage its own credibility? Like all humans, we are always going to make mistakes. The goal is to try to avoid them and to acknowledge and correct them as quickly as possible…And I think we will be less willing simply to show speeches without fact-checking and context."

The *Columbia Journalism Review* published an in-depth article by Pete Vernon quoting *Politico*'s Jack Shafer. It advocates a middle ground for journalists who are evaluating whether to report untruthful political rhetoric delivered at rallies or disseminated online. "In the past, we didn't think every presidential speech was newsworthy—when he was speaking to the Boy Scouts or to a sewing circle. It was news but it was 'small news'…I think we have to deal on the merits. There is no obligation to cover them all, and no obligation to ignore them either…I would say reporters have to go and find news where it is, and sometimes it's Twitter, sometimes it's not."

Shafer believes, "Twitter is part of a president's publicity apparatus, and it should be considered [official] just like press releases, public appearances, and photo ops."[143]

All administrations aspire to take control of the narrative and spoon-feed their message to the press and the public. Energetic and enterprising journalists look below the surface to tell us something we don't know, something our leaders may not want us to know. Often the best way to break those stories is confidential sources. In coming decades, will the conservative-leaning Supreme Court uphold or overturn laws governing the protection of sources? Jonathan Peters warns, "There is no federal shield law and the First Amendment offers highly inconsistent protections against compelled disclosure of sources and materials...Yet the federal government has subpoenaed numerous journalists in the past twenty years to try to compel them to testify about their confidential sources...This is a critical problem calling out for legislative action."[144] Congressional debate on this issue may be necessary, but it could degenerate into an ideological free-for-all, with opponents of the press trying to settle scores and silence critics.

While he agrees that protecting the identity of confidential sources is paramount, *NBC Nightly News* anchor Lester Holt believes, "It's about transparency. I do think it's healthy that people become critical thinkers and question what they read and some of what they see. But, from our perspective, we combat that by being more transparent, talking more about how we source our stories. We don't rely generally on a single source. Telling people as much as we can about the process where this information comes from...is something we do on a normal basis, but in this time of heightened skepticism, we can't do it enough."[145]

Looking back, will we learn valuable lessons? Media giants are weighing options and questioning the way they do business. One essential tool of the trade is access—knowing the right people and ingratiating yourself so officials cooperate when you're on deadline. Katy Tur of NBC and MSNBC is reevaluating the way she views access. "I've been thinking a lot about access lately. Access is seductive. Access means good nuggets from a campaign. Access means your phone calls are answered. Access is safe and secure because you're the one at your organization who can always get a comment, a confirmation, or an exclusive interview. But access journalism is barely journalism. And somewhere along the way...I decided access journalism isn't worth it."[146]

Thoughtful reflections about the direction of broadcast news must also address the question of bias. Viewer surveys reveal that fewer and fewer news outlets pass the test. Ted Koppel agrees that outlets for the unvarnished truth are limited. "NPR quite clearly is more liberal than conservative. But they strive manfully to maintain a balance and to inform the listening public. Programs like *Frontline* do an extraordinary job. And the documentaries that are available that you can find on cable television these days, many of them on HBO, many of them on outfits like Netflix...are doing brilliant work. But when it comes to radio and television—PBS, NPR, BBC. Not a whole lot else...I guess if I'm going to leave you with any single thought, it is the support for old-fashioned, objective, fact-based, middle-of-the-road journalism. Not that it'll do away with right-wing journalism or left-wing journalism. But there has to be something there for the average American voter who doesn't necessarily feel drawn to either extreme and simply wants to know what's going on in this world. I used to have a boss many, many years ago by the name of Av Westin. He was an executive producer of the evening news. And Av would say to us, 'What I want to know and what our viewers and listeners need to know is: Is the world safe? Is my country safe? Is my home safe? We've got to start answering those questions again.'"[147]

And what about the role of new media and its future impact? During the Trump administration, the internet and blogosphere exploded with a multitude of alternative sites. Koppel makes this observation. "When I was a young journalist, if you wanted to go into broadcasting, you had three options: ABC, NBC, CBS. There was no cable. There was no satellite. There was no internet. These days, anyone with a laptop computer has the capacity of being able to reach hundreds, thousands, potentially tens of thousands of people. And what is it that drives the number up? The number of clicks. To a large extent, it is the level of outrage…that you're able to engender among your audience. It's not fact based. It doesn't need to be. In fact, sometimes, that's nothing but an impediment. To the extent that you can get people really angry, they will be clicking on. And as they click, you begin to make money and get more circulation. The business of journalism is undermined. I don't know what the answer is to that part of it."[148]

Derek Thompson believes, "It is either narcissistic or outdated, or both, for media organizations to pretend that they have a monopoly on the power to amplify news. In the mid-twentieth century, this might have been a realistic notion. But the sum total of social media, podcasts, newsletters, and the whole international cacophony of information exchange has entirely swamped the establishment in power and reach. Four times as many Americans saw Russian-influenced content on Facebook [about 130 million] than own a print or digital subscription to an American newspaper [31 million]. Foreign interference will likely remain a serious threat, one of the complex factors disrupting our traditional campaign process."[149]

Mika Brzezinski of MSNBC's *Morning Joe* has stern words for digital giants. "Facebook needs to understand that it's a news organization or a media organization. I think that there are many constructs out there—search engines, whatever you want to call them—and they've all become a part of this strange strainer that is the way people get news. We don't get news the way people did when we were growing up. Now, it's just everywhere and you don't even know what's news and what's not. People search things and think that's news. They have no concept of how to collate this stuff. We're in for a rough ride over the next two decades, trying to get to the other side of this where there's some parameter in place or regulation. I'm not really sure what it's going to look like, but this is going to come to a head and it's going to get worse, where either it'll lead to violence or something that is caused by misinformation. We're going to have to install some parameters in what is the wild west of internet news, information sites, and search engines."[150]

"The rise of digital media has empowered people worldwide and enabled the spread of misinformation and demagoguery and undermined the funding of professional journalism...The move from a media environment defined by broadcasting and newspapers to digital, mobile, and platform environments is the most fundamental change in how we communicate since the development of the printing press." That analysis comes from Oxford professor Rasmus Kleis Nielsen. "Media companies still create the news agenda, but platform companies control access to audiences...This move to digital media and platforms does not generate filter bubbles but more diverse news diets...The automated serendipity of social media feeds search engine results...and drives people to more and more diverse sources of information…that they do not seek out of their own volition."[151]

Even people trying to avoid the news aren't immune from digital bombardment. During election cycles, unwanted text messages and emails are the preferred means of instantaneous communication. It may be the cheapest form of campaign outreach ever invented. One click and you can reach masses of potential voters. In addition, legitimate media outlets send urgent text alerts as news develops. In the past, ultimate power rested with the consumer who could act like an ostrich or seek out the latest news on their personal timetable via radio, television, newspapers, or magazines. Now there's no escape from incoming digital headlines that are perfectly crafted for short-attention-span consumers. As digital media expand their stronghold, their corporate profiles and profits will increase at the expense of once-powerful news outlets that will watch their influence steadily erode and their profits steadily decline. That raises a provocative question. Is it possible the media bottom line will miss Donald Trump when he vacates 1600 Pennsylvania Avenue? Is it possible that with an ordinary president in the White House, the daily drama will end, ratings will level off, and revenues will drop?

Conservative columnist Cal Thomas thinks it's time for media to "engage in serious introspection…Journalism is a business. Think of it this way. If you owned a gas station and were losing customers because gas prices were too high, the lighting was poor so people felt unsafe at night, and the restrooms were dirty—would you allow those conditions to persist if a competitor opened a station across the street with lower prices, better lighting, and cleaner restrooms? Not if you wanted to stay in business, you wouldn't. Too many media are like the guy who owns the substandard gas station, ignoring complaints about their performance. The predictable results are fewer readers of newspapers and lower ratings for television news programs. What should frighten all of us is the latest survey of people who expect their loss of faith in the media to be permanent."[152]

An emphasis on quality journalism could mitigate the loss of faith. Scott Pelley of CBS *60 Minutes* thinks, "The dividing line that matters now is the one between journalism and junk. The 2016 presidential campaign was the first in our history in which citizens were awash in false stories masquerading as news. Much of this disinformation campaign was engineered by domestic political partisans and by Russia."[153]

Andrea Mitchell has been a voice of reason throughout her career. "I think we'll never get back to that [old] brand of retail politics because of the Trump phenomenon…and the mainstream media, all of us, social media, got swept up in it way too much. I think we have a lot to answer for with the way we covered the [2016] campaign. I hope we can get away from this kind of campaigning and get back to something that is more closely approaching a real conversation with the American people that has to do with policies, subjects like education and housing and climate change and all the other things we should be covering."[154]

Washington Post media columnist Margaret Sullivan believes acknowledging past mistakes could benefit future campaign coverage. "Well, I hope we will learn some lessons from this…I think we do need to be doing some self-examination about the role we played in further dividing the country by giving Donald Trump a platform and an unquestioning one at times. I don't know what television journalism is going to look like, but I hope we will take some lessons and apply them."

Media obsession with the horse race rather than the issues allows the most colorful candidates to control the dialogue and shift attention from substance to personality. Political personalities aren't the only distraction. Some journalists or "pseudo-journalists" hunger for the spotlight and hijack the story by injecting themselves into the headlines. "Trump leads in the self-promotion sweepstakes, but the press is close behind. Journalistic prize culture has shaped professional media, with some journalists developing a celebrity of their own…making themselves more important than the story. This widens the gap between the press and the people, who see journalists moving in the same circles as stars and politicians, including the likes of Trump."[155]

Scott Pelley has an interesting take. "Our credibility is damaged when reporters reach for fame rather than public service. It has become common for reporters to appear in movies and fictional dramas. One night the reporter is relaying election results on a news program, the next night you encounter him in a movie reporting on the invasion of aliens from space. This desire for personal fame is the same instinct that leads some reporters to embellish their reporting or embellish their role in reporting. To them, it's more important to be celebrated than believed. Reporters who grasp for fame have forgotten that journalism has nothing to do with being popular."[156]

To what degree will the current crop of journalism majors be seduced by the celebrity factor? When I was hiring young staffers at television networks, I was immediately turned off by anyone who uttered the words, "I've always wanted to be on television." Wrong answer. It's about the story, not about you. Dr. Patrick L. Plaisance, PhD, cautions, "In communications programs around the country, a new gospel of 'entrepreneurial journalism' has taken hold…Aspiring reporters and producers are being told to focus on cultivating their own brand. On one level, this makes perfect sense.

Writers and editors are entering a deeply fragmented market in which a spot in the newsroom of a major metro daily or a network affiliate is no longer the norm. Individual voices can now command huge online audiences. But when the logical extension of this focus on journalists' branding points to super brands…mixing journalism with celebrity will inevitably result in a toxic brew."[157]

Landing a highly sought-after exclusive interview is a reliable way for a reporter to get attention. Maybe it's time we reexamine the prized "exclusive"—not the process of getting it, but the process of labeling it on air. Competition is fierce. I get that, but sometimes an "exclusive" is not really all that special. Hypothetically, let's suppose a morning show on a broadcast network scores a legit one-on-one exclusive with the newsmaker of the moment. Like an out-of-control tidal wave, other programs follow suit later in the day, hyping the "leftovers" with banners that scream "CABLE News Exclusive" or "PRIMETIME Exclusive." They're playing with linguistics and shading the truth. Their exclusive is rehash, not groundbreaking. We already saw the real exclusive on the morning show. Reporters don't make those calls unilaterally. Experienced producers trying to save face and boost ratings often do, and by osmosis young staffers absorb the wrong message.

Frank Sesno has sage advice for aspiring journalists now and in the future. "My advice. Do the job. Stay focused. Don't be distracted or drawn into diversionary tactics that newsmakers or news organizations dangle out there every day. In November 2018, the climate report was released on Black Friday when the public is consuming less news than just about any day of the year. But several media organizations determined there was enough in that report to pursue it for days and weeks after, to not let a huge story be buried…Journalists in this very tense time must go out of their way to resist the drug of ratings and clicks and recognize the larger journalistic and public responsibility to cover the news. I would pursue a thread of 'explanatory journalism' where I clearly lay out policy, implications, contradictions, and cost. I would lean towards coverage in a series of stories so that I could come at the issues in depth, detail, and variety. I would get outside of Washington and cross the country to hear from people who are being affected by the big issues. Separately, I'd certainly keep track of the misstatements, falsehoods, accusations, and inconsistencies so that the president—like all others in power—is held accountable for his words, deeds, and the impact of his policies."

Legendary journalist Gay Talese passes along time-tested advice he received as a cub reporter. "Stay off the telephone. Show up in person. No matter how inconvenient it may be, always meet face-to-face…Look people in the eye. Observe everything firsthand. Be there…I sometimes refer to my method as the 'Art of Hanging Out.'"[158] Good advice in a fast-paced digital world dominated by emails and Google searches.

CNN's Anderson Cooper urges his successors to be self-reliant and self-confident. His advice is a twenty-first-century version of Polonius's admonition—to thine own self be true. "You all have something that is unique and different, and don't let somebody in a newsroom who's been in the profession for forty years squeeze that out of you and make you sound like everybody else who's in the newsroom."[159]

Ted Koppel cautions the new wave of journalists, "I would say that a democracy, a system like ours cannot survive in the long run without fact-based, honest journalism. We can't do without it. And to the extent that we seem to be drifting away from that model, to the extent that we have anything less than fact-based journalism, our system is in peril. So, I urge you, by all means, keep studying, keep working, get a job with a good bunch of journalists as fast as you can…Learn the trade. We have never needed it more."[160]

But when aspiring young reporters try to break into the business, they may find that opportunities are severely limited. Jeff Greenfield cites a troubling statistic. "If you want to know just how devastating things are in the journalism business, I believe the employment rate among daily journalists at newspapers in America is down by about something like forty percent in the last fifteen to twenty years. If you walk into a major newspaper—and I've had this experience in Columbus and I've had it in Cleveland, Philadelphia. These once-cavernous newsrooms, you could shoot a canon off and not hit anybody."[161]

I had a similar experience at the *Miami Herald* a number of years ago when I interviewed Dave Barry at the old headquarters downtown. Large portions of the newsroom were dark with rows and rows of empty desks. No computers, no telephones, no photos or mementos, no leftover coffee cups, no fast food wrappers. It was a ghost town.

The coronavirus pandemic proved fatal for some local newspapers unable to survive the plague without ad revenue. Other newspapers are firing more reporters than they're hiring. NYU journalism professor Mitchell Stephens points out, "If the main goal of a twenty-first-century journalism organization is to fill its site with wisdom, the hiring practices at most American news organizations have not been changing fast enough…The career ladder in journalism has often seemed as encrusted with tradition as the stories.

It has been hard to let go of the expectation that you should work your way up through a series of beats...Experienced practitioners in any field tend to advise or require newcomers to replicate their own career paths. But in journalism, with newspapers and broadcast stations laying off more than hiring, that old path is disappearing. And if [my] view of where journalism is heading is correct, that path no longer seems to proceed in the right direction for gathering facts and interpreting them, which are two different activities...And twenty-first-century journalists need to learn how to interpret."[162]

Media scholar C.W. Anderson has a novel idea. He calls for replacing "beats with obsessions, the patterns, trends, and seismic shifts that are shaping the world our readers live in...It is, in short, a gamble that the public can rise to the occasion, figure things out, and act upon that knowledge. In today's world of collapsing journalistic business models, new social movements, and new technologies for democratic accountability, it may be a gamble worth taking. At least, it may be the only option left."[163]

Many journalists who've worked a designated beat disagree with scrapping the system. True, a general assignment reporter can parachute into the transit agency, the homicide bureau, or the corporate boardroom without historical context or sources. They'll get the story, but without the insight that comes with knowing the power brokers and seeing events in a continuum. Because beat reporters know the players, they don't have to start the process by introducing themselves. Comparing journalism to medicine, political reporters differ from environmental reporters the way orthopedists differ from cardiologists. And from management's point of view, beats are a logical way to organize personnel and budgets.

Michael Riley, writing for neimanreports.org, argues, "In recent years, the beat has become the Rodney Dangerfield of journalism. It just doesn't get the respect it deserves. That approach, however, is about to undergo a radical transformation as journalism, searching desperately for its future, begins to discover, once again, the profound value of expertise, exclusivity, and depth. Those elements, it turns out, imbue content with value...The next wave of journalistic progress will channel its power from the underlying principle of the reporter's beat: the creation by an expert of valuable content that readers need and can't find anywhere else. This proper emphasis on expertise promises to give rise to subscription-based business models in which people will pay for exclusive content they value. It's a way to resolve the question dogging journalists as they search for resources to fund reporting. Unless readers recognize value in what they are getting, they are unwilling to pay for its production."[164]

Rasmus Kleis Nielsen observes, "The business models that fund news are challenged, weakening professional journalism and leaving news media more vulnerable to commercial and political pressures...The risk here is not simply retrenchment and less coverage of many important issues...A less robust business of journalism is more vulnerable to media capture by the state or politically motivated owners and to pressure from advertisers...As the business of news changes, journalism also risks becoming less robust and ultimately incapable of helping the public make sense of our times. This challenge is compounded by increasingly open political hostility towards independent professional journalism, and in the worst case, a veritable war on journalism."[165]

As Frank Sesno looks ahead to the future of journalism, he says, "We talk a lot about how the media should change, how politicians attack the media, how all of this undermines public trust and institutions. But we need to point back at us as citizens as well. Now, more than ever in the course of human history, ordinary citizens have access to information and voices that not long ago would have been inconceivable. News consumers have a new responsibility to seek news and information that informs before it enflames. They need to understand what's at stake, where credible information can be found, how they can recognize and check it. News consumers need to understand that they share responsibility for consuming as healthy an information diet as a food diet. Junk food abounds. It is cheaper, easier, and often more fun to consume than health food. But our health and our hearts require a balanced diet."

Chris Matthews believes, "People need to get the news from several sources. They need to be the final editor of what they believe. They need to retain their belief in objective fact. Opinion must be based on recognizable truth...My first job in journalism was delivering the *Philadelphia Bulletin*. People read it in the late afternoon and evening to get all the great columnists. They wanted to know what they thought of the day's events and politics. Now primetime cable fills a similar role." But will that role thrive in a generational shift as millennial voters look to digital sources to assess the players and policies that will shape their futures?

Taking the digital revolution a step further, producers and TV executives may lose their discretionary power as viewers start to program their own newscasts. Viewers can already watch news on demand, constructing their own rundowns by selecting which stories to watch and which to skip. TV coverage will simulate a news buffet, emphasizing freedom of choice. *Yes* to the presidential debate, the World Series, and the plane crash. *No thanks* to Madonna and the transit strike in a distant city.

Pulitzer Prize winner Seymour Hersh admits, "I do not pretend to have an answer to the problems of our media today...This is clearly the time to renew the debate on how to go forward...And there is no magic bullet, no savior in sight for serious media. The mainstream newspapers, magazines and television networks will continue to lay off reporters, reduce staff, and squeeze the funds available for good reporting and especially for investigative reporting."[166]

Writing in *Vanity Fair*, Peter Hamby suggests "packaging news in ways that grab attention and reward the consumer. It demands investment and creativity and a willingness to abandon cherished J-school lesson plans." He cites Snapchat, the digital platform for NBC's daily feed *Stay Tuned*. It was "created deliberately for the vertical screen mobile experience, averaged between 25 and 35 million unique viewers per month in September 2018 with a core audience that watches several times a week. About seventy-five percent of the *Stay Tuned* audience is under twenty-five—an elusive but massive demographic that may never ever watch a news show on linear television."[167]

Hamby interviewed MIT Researcher Hossein Derakhshan, who thinks "journalism" needs to be decoupled from "news" in order to save itself. "Here's what that means. Think of news as just the device for delivering the hard work of journalism: the reporting, facts, information, and commentary. [That's journalism.] News, meanwhile, is just the container, the package, the website, the newspaper, the TV show, the radio broadcast...Many millions find these experiences tedious and irrelevant, a realization that has given rise to the morning email newsletter, the listicle, or the well-turned piece of digital video. All of these formats are creative reimaginings of journalism redesigned to match how consumers live today. As in politics, the messenger matters...The truth is that the news is dying, but journalism will not and should not."[168]

Part of the reinvention process may result from generational divides within the newsroom. "Younger journalists and journalists of color who understand emerging formats should be empowered to coach their veteran colleagues into not being so precious about their treasured models of storytelling. And, in a convenient trade, maybe those old fogeys can give the younger set a few books about things that happened in politics before the year 2016. Once the political class better understands the shifting habits of Americans in an age of fracturing attention, we'll figure out how to tell better stories and create journalism in ways that engage people and feel worthy of their time, even if those stories look and sound different than the ones we were taught in journalism class."[169]

When Frank Sesno looks into the crystal ball, he believes, "We can't put the genie back in the bottle again. We've entered an era of more personal, more conscientious politics and journalism. But there will be a great hunger for responsible and unifying figures. That's an opportunity for a new generation of political leaders— and a new generation of journalists and communicators. It will be noisy, competitive, disaggregated. We will never again have 'Uncle Walter' as the prevailing voice of news. But there are huge opportunities for journalists who are perceptive, informative, great storytellers, and believe passionately in the mission of journalism to inform and engage."

The times may be changing, but the passion of journalists remains the same. Christiane Amanpour says, "I would give women and men the same advice—follow your heart, follow your gut, follow your instincts. Journalism is about adherence to the truth. That's what you're going to report—you're going to find facts, the truth, and you're going to be the eyes and ears of folks back home who need and want to know what's going on in the world."[170]

Lester Holt is optimistic about the future of journalism. "There are so many moving parts. There are so many norms being challenged, not only on the political level, but other areas of life. Everything is coming at us at ninety miles per hour. And people really want a port in the storm every night and we try to provide that...Those voices that try and talk us down only make us more determined to carry out our mission as journalists. We firmly believe that what we do is an important pillar of a healthy functioning democracy, and we will always stand for it."[171]

Framers of the Constitution never envisioned our brave new world of television or the internet when they crafted the First Amendment. But they prioritized freedom of the press, ranking it one of the most essential tenets of our fledgling democracy. Their intent was clear. "Congress shall make no law...abridging the freedom of speech or of the press." Adherence to that cherished American principle is under attack as journalists wage an existential battle that we as a nation cannot afford to lose.

Edward R. Murrow gets the last word. "We must not confuse dissent with disloyalty. When the loyal opposition dies, I think the soul of America dies with it...To be persuasive, we must be believable. To be believable, we must be credible. To be credible, we must be truthful."[172] Amen to that.

ENDNOTES

1 Jim Acosta, *The Enemy of the People*

2 Ted Koppel & Jeff Greenfield, 92nd Street Y New York, April 28, 2019

3 Chris Cuomo, *The Late Show with Steven Colbert*, CBS, May 2, 2019

4 Rudolph Giuliani, *Meet the Press*, NBC, August 19, 2019

5 Newton Minnow, *Chicago Tribune*, March 12, 2019

6 April Ryan, *Erin Burnett Out Front*, CNN, April 18, 2019

7 Paige Williams, *The New Yorker*, September 24, 2018

8 Max Boot, *Reliable Sources*, CNN June 16, 2019

9 Jim Acosta, *The Enemy of the People*

10 Matthew Yglesias, VOX, October 31, 2018

11 Katy Tur, *Unbelievable*

12 Jeff Zucker, *Reliable Sources*, CNN, October 27, 2019

13 Jim Acosta, *The Enemy of the People*

14 Scott Pelley, *Truth Worth Telling*

15 Derek Thompson, *The Atlantic* November 19, 2018

16 Ibid.

17 Don Lemon, 92nd Street Y New York, June 9, 2019

18 Chris Cuomo, Ibid

19 George Lakoff, quoted by Derek Thompson, *The Atlantic* November 28, 2018

20 Matthew Ingram, *Columbia Journalism Review*, October 10, 2018

21 Pete Vernon, *Columbia Journalism Review*, October 10, 2018

22 Brian Stelter, quoted by Pete Vernon, *Columbia Journalism Review*, Fall 2017

23 David Zurawik, *Reliable, Sources*, CNN, July 28, 2019

24 April Ryan, *Reliable Sources*, CNN, July 28, 2019

25 Brian Stelter, *Reliable Sources*, CNN, November 25, 2018

26 Jeff Greenfield & Ted Koppel, 92 Street Y New York, April 28, 2019

27 Brian Stelter, *Reliable Sources*, CNN, December 9, 2018

28 Jim Acosta, *The Enemy of the People*

29 Shorenstein Center on Media, Harvard's Kennedy School, December 7, 2016

30 Katy Tur, *Unbelievable*

31 Scott Pelley, *Truth Worth Telling*

32 Jim Acosta, *The Enemy of the People*

33 Lara Logan, *Mike Drop* & *The New York Post*

34 Chris Cuomo, *The Late Show with Stephen Colbert*, CBS, June 9, 2019

35 Lara Logan, the *New York Post*, February 26, 2019

36 Jeff Greenfield & Ted Koppel, 92 Street Y, April 28, 2019

37 Ibid

38 Seymour Hersh, *Reporter*

39 Lara Logan, *The New York Post*, February 26, 2019

40 Katy Tur, *Unbelievable*

41 Ted Koppel, 92 Street Y New York, April 28, 2019

42 Neil Cavuto, *Your World with Neil Cavuto*, FNC, May 3, 2018

43 Rick Wilson, *Morning Joe*, MSNBC, October 29, 2018

44 Jim Acosta, *The Enemy of the People*

45 Ted Koppel, 92 Street Y New York, April 28, 2019

46 Lara Logan, *New York Post*, February 26, 2018

47 Katy Tur, *Unbelievable*

48 Ben Shapiro, *Reliable Sources*, CNN, May 5, 2019

49 Ted Koppel & Jeff Greenfield, 92 Street Y New York, April 28, 2019

50 Ibid

51 Jim Acosta, *The Enemy of the People*

52 Kyle Pope, *Columbia Journalism Review*, January 22, 2018

53 Jim Acosta, *The Enemy of the People*

54 Tucker Carlson, *Tucker Carlson Tonight*, FNC, December 3, 2018

55 Andrea Mitchell, 92 Street Y New York, November 20, 2018

56 Jeff Greenfield & Ted Koppel, 92 Street Y New York, April 28, 2019

57 Anderson Cooper, speech, Arizona State University, October 17, 2018

58 Jeffrey Toobin, CNN

59 Vince Lombardi and Henry Russell Sanders

60 Andrea Mitchell, 92 Street Y New York, November 20, 2018

61 Jim Acosta, *Enemy of the People*

62 Sarah Sanders, *Deadline*, November 13, 2018

63 Chris Wallace, *Daily Briefing*, FNC, November 8, 2018

64 CNN Statement, *Variety*, November 13, 2018

65 Jay Wallace, *FoxNews.com*, November 14, 2018

66 Andrea Mitchell, 92 Street Y New York, November 20, 2018

67 Lara Logan, *New York Post*, February 26, 201

68 David Gergen, Commonwealth Club, San Francisco, July 24, 2018

69 Jim Acosta, *The Enemy of the People*

70 Bill Kristol, CNN, October 2018

71 Mika Bzrezinski, *Morning Joe*, MSNBC, October 2018

72 Scott Pelley, *Truth Worth Telling*

73 April Ryan, *The Hill*, June 4, 2019

74 Jim Acosta, *The Enemy of The People*

75 Katie Tur, *Unbelievable*

76 Ibid

77 Ibid

78 Ken Vogel, Twitter, August 20, 2018

79 David Gergen, CNN

80 Fox Statement, *Politico*, November 6, 2019

81 Jill Lepore, *New Yorker*, quoting *Forbes.com*, January 28, 2019

82 Kyle Pope, *Columbia Journalism Review*, January 22, 2018

83 *Sunday Morning*, CBS, March 26,2017

84 Ibid

85 Ted Koppel, 92 Street Y New York, April 28, 2019

86 Ibid

87 Walter Cronkite, *CBS Evening News*, February 27, 1968

88 Joel Achenbach,,*The Washington Post* May 25, 2018

89 Ted Koppel, 92 Street Y New York, April 28, 2019

90 Kenneth T. Walsh, *U.S. News and World Report*, February 2018

91 Jack Mirkinson, *Huffington Post*, March 17, 2014

92 Michael J. Arlen, *The Atlantic*, 1972

93 Google, *This Day in History*

94 David Brock & Ari Rabin-Havt, *The FOX Effect*

95 Ted Koppel, 92 Street Y New York, April 28, 2019

96 Toby Miller, University of California, 2004

97 David Brock & Ari Rabin-Havt, *The FOX Effect*

98 Ibid

99 Ibid

100 Ibid

101 Jack Shafer, *Slate*, quoting David Foster Wallace

102 Reece Peck, CUNY professor

103 David Brock & Ari Rabin-Havt, *The FOX Effect*

104 Jacob L. Nelson, *Columbia Journalism Review*, quoting Lauren Feldman and Andy Guess, January 23, 2019

105 Pat King, *Metro USA*, May 9, 2019

106 Change.org

107 Connor Schoen, *Harvard Political Review*, October 30, 2017

108 Brian Stelter, *Reliable Sources*, CNN, July 28, 2019

109 Ted Koppel, 92 Street Y New York, April 28, 2019

110 A.R. Lakshmanan, Poynter Institute, September 1, 2017

111 Marc Gunther, *The Neiman Report*

112 Paul Waldman, *The American Prospect*, February 13, 2015

113 KK Ottesen, *The Washington Post*, July 23, 2019

114 Tom Jones, Poynter Institute, May 2, 2019

115 Norah O'Donnell, *CBS Evening News*, July 15, 2019

116 Ted Koppel, 92 Street Y New York, April 28, 2019

117 Jeff Greenfield, 92 Street Y New York, April 28, 2019

118 Pew Research Center Report, 2004

119 Rand Corporation Report, May 12, 2019

120 Ibid

121 Katie Tur, *Unbelievable*

122 Ted Koppel, 92 Street Y New York, April 28, 2019

123 Neiman Reports, Special Edition, 1999

124 Ibid

125 Ted Koppel, 92 Street Y New York, April 28, 2019

126 Katie Tur, *Unbelievable*

127 Mark Damazer, BBC News Editorial Policy

128 Jill Geisler, *The Poynter Center Report*, May 2, 2011

129 Pew Research Center, July 10, 2006

130 Seymour Hersh, *Reporter*

131 Pew Research Center, July 10, 2006

132 Ibid

133 Ibid

134 Ted Koppel, 92 Street Y New York, April 28, 2019

135 Pew Research Center, July 10, 2006

136 Ibid

137 Ted Koppel, 92 Street Y New York, April 28, 2019

138 Senator John McCain, *Meet the Press*, NBC, February 18, 2017

139 Jim Acosta, *The Enemy of the People*

140 Ted Koppel, 92 Street Y New York, April 28, 2019

141 Mitchell Stephens, *Beyond News: The Future of Journalism*

142 Brian Stelter, *Reliable Sources* CNN, July 14, 2019

143 Jack Shafer, quoted by Pete Vernon, *Columbia Journalism Review*, Fall 2017

144 Jonathan Peters, *Columbia Journalism Review*, August 22, 2016

145 Tom Jones, the Poynter Institute, May 2, 2019

146 Katy Tur, *Unbelievable*

147 Ted Koppel, 92 Street Y New York, April 28, 2019

148 Ibid

149 Derek Thompson, *The New Yorker*, May 1, 2019

150 Connor Schoen, *Harvard Political Review*, October 30, 2017

151 Rasmus Kleis Nielsen, Twitter, January 23, 2019

152 Cal Thomas, Syndicated Column, June 28, 2019

153 Scott Pelley, *Truth Worth Telling*

154 Andrea Mitchell, 92 Street Y New York, November 20, 2018

155 Robert E. Gutsche Jr., Online Post

156 Scott Pelley, *Truth Worth Telling*

157 Dr. Patrick L. Plaisance Ph.D., *Psychology Today*, March 25, 2015

158 Gay Talese, *Columbia Journalism Review*, August 14, 2017

159 Anderson Cooper, Speech, Cronkite Awards, Columbia University

160 Ted Koppel, 92 Street Y New York, April 28, 2019

161 Jeff Greenfield, 92 Street Y New York, April 28, 2019

162 Mitchell Stephens, *Beyond News: The Future of Journalism*

163 C. W. Anderson, Neimanlab.org, September 20, 2012

164 Michael Riley, Neimanreports.org, January 10, 2011

165 Rasmus Kleis Nielsen, Twitter, January 23, 2019

166 Seymour Hersh, *Reporter*

167 Peter Hamby, *Vanity Fair*, January 24, 2019

168 Ibid

169 Ibid

170 Lisa Ryan, *New York* magazine, April 10, 2018

171 Tom Jones, the Poynter Institute, May 2, 2019

172 Edward R. Murrow, *See It Now*, CBS March 9, 1954

INDEX

A

Abby Phillip 51
Achenbach, Joel 63, 127
Acosta, Jim 2, 6, 9, 18, 21, 28, 31, 33, 39, 40, 41, 46, 52, 105, 125, 126, 127, 129
Ailes, Roger 68, 70, 75
Alcindor, Yamiche 51
Amanpour, Christiane 81, 122
Anderson, C.W. 118
Aristotle 36
Arlen, Michael J. 66, 127
Axelrod, David 81

B

Baier, Bret 27, 45, 74
Barnicle, Mike 80, 101
Baron, Marty 42
Barr, William 35
Barry, Dave 117
Bash, Dana 81
Beck, Glenn 72
Bee, Samantha 36
Berman, John 81, 101
Bernstein, Carl 67, 81
Beschloss, Michael 80
Bettag, Tom 100
Beutel, Bill 69
Bill O'Reilly 75
bin Salman, Mohammad 34
Bolduan, Kate 11, 81
Boot, Max 5, 27, 28, 125
Borger, Gloria 81
Bradlee, Ben 83
Bradley, Bill 69
Brawley, Tawana 69
Brinkley, David 67, 87
Brock, David 72, 76, 127, 128

Graham, Lindsey 26
Gralnick, Jeff 99, 102
Greenfield, Jeff 3, 17, 23, 30, 36, 90, 100, 117, 125, 126, 128, 129
Griffin, Phil 79
Grimsby, Roger 69

H

Haberman, Maggie 81
Hamby, Peter 121, 130
Hannity, Sean 50, 56, 57, 59, 74, 83
Harlow, Poppy 46
Harrison, George 36
Hawley, Josh 56
Heilemann, John 80
Herblock 36
Hersh, Seymour 24, 99, 120, 126, 129, 130
Holt, Lester 18, 88, 108, 122
Huckabee, Mike 73
Hume, Brit 29, 57
Huntley, Chet 87

I

Ignatius, David 80
Ingraham, Laura 48, 57
Ingram, Matthew 125
Isaacson, Walter 80

J

Jefferson, Thomas 6, 37, 43
Jennings, Peter 87, 88, 98
Johnson, Lyndon B. 65

K

Kasich, John 26
Kayyem, Juliette 81
Kelly, Megyn 75
Kennedy, Bobby 65
Kennedy, John F. 83
Khashoggi, Jamal 34
Kim, Jong-un 56
Klieman, Rikki 101
Koch, Ed 69, 94
Koppel, Ted 3, 11, 17, 23, 26, 29, 30, 36, 59, 64, 71, 84, 89, 92, 93, 100, 103,

O

P

R

S

V

W

Y

Z

CPSIA information can be obtained
at www.ICGtesting.com
Printed in the USA
LVHW080711010920
664669LV00029B/1552